GW00949972

Picture librarianship

OUTLINES OF MODERN LIBRARIANSHIP

Titles included in the series are

OUTLINES OF MODERN LIBRARIANSHIP

Picture librarianship

Hilary Evans

K · G · Saur  Clive Bingley

New York · London · München · Paris

First published 1980
by Clive Bingley Ltd, a member of
the K G Saur International Publishing Group.
Copyright © Hilary Evans.
Set in 11 on 12 point Baskerville by Allset.
Printed and bound in the UK by
Redwood Burn Ltd of Trowbridge and Esher.
Bingley (UK) ISBN: 0-85157-294-4
Saur (USA) ISBN: 0-89664-428-6

British Library Cataloguing in Publication Data

Evans, Hilary
    Picture librarianship. - (Outlines of modern
    librarianship).
    1. Libraries - Special collections - Pictures
    2. Library administration
    I. Title   II. Series
    025.17'71   Z692.P5

    ISBN 0-85157-294-4

CONTENTS

PREFACE

THE VERY phrase 'picture library' is a contradiction in terms. The word 'library' indicates a place where books are kept, not pictures or gramophone records or documents. Pictures may be kept in an archive, perhaps, or a gallery or a print room or even a photothèque; but a library should be a place for books.

However, the phrase, with all its ambiguity, is doubtless here to stay. We must learn to live with the built-in paradox and accept 'picture libraries' along with 'record libraries' and 'map libraries'. But the point is more than one of dryasdust pedantry. There is a good reason for recognising the anomaly, and keeping it continually in mind. We must not let the paradox fool us into thinking that a picture library is the same as a book library—or picture librarianship the same as book librarianship—only with pictures in the place of books.

Rather, the picture librarian will be well advised to regard his occupation as radically different from that of his colleague in the world of books. Instead of starting with the skills of book librarianship and modifying them when necessary to the handling of pictures, he should regard picture librarianship as a skill-system in its own right; parallel to, rather than deriving from, book librarianship. Let him by all means draw on book librarianship for guidance when circumstances are appropriate, for with its age superiority of over two thousand years, book librarianship possesses a heritage of accumulated wisdom on which every later comer into archivery will wish to draw. But he must not let himself be overawed by that august lineage, rather, be prepared to flout its rules and draw up his own to meet his own needs.

Such will be the guiding principle adopted in the pages

which follow. It is assumed that the reader has some knowledge of the basic principles of how libraries work, though perhaps only from using them rather than working in them: no formal qualifications or even practical experience in librarianship are assumed. Should the reader be so fortunate as to possess such qualifications or such experience, he is advised to set them temporarily on one side, and to approach picture librarianship as a discipline in its own right, with its own specific problems and its own specific solutions. Only when these have been recognised and evaluated, as problems and solutions pertaining uniquely to picture librarianship, can it be seen what experience gained elsewhere will be useful or relevant.

It will then be found that the picture librarian is a special kind of person. Perhaps any competent book librarian could prove himself reasonably competent also as a picture librarian; but to achieve something better than competence, something more than book-library skills are needed. The book librarian who contemplates transferring to the world of pictures must be prepared to revise his outlook and open his mind to a new way of looking at the material for which he is responsible and the way it is used.

The book you are about to read will show, more than anything else, how unique a profession picture librarianship is—uniquely challenging, uniquely rewarding. To be successful, the picture librarian must possess a correspondingly unique spectrum of skills and faculties. And first and foremost of these, he must be truly at home in the world of pictures—love them, feel them, read them, as a book librarian loves and feels and reads books. Even more than books, because the language of the picture is more immediate than that of the written word, pictures are the records of human experience, human feelings, human imagination. The way in which a picture is made, every facet of its technique and composition, is eloquent of its creator's personality, his attitudes and values, his intentions, his social background and the *zeitgeist* within whose parameters he worked. Over and above any of the technical skills described in these pages, the picture librarian must be aware of pictures as vehicles of communication, visual documents each with its own uniquely

8

revealing message. For it is the storing and preserving and passing on of these messages that picture librarianship is all about.

ONE

THE NATURE AND FUNCTION
OF THE PICTURE LIBRARY

A PICTURE library is a collection of pictures, collected for some purpose or for personal satisfaction, but usually following some guiding principle which dictates either the scope of the material or the uses to which that material is to be put. While some picture collections may originally have been formed simply to gratify a collector's whim, it is not with such collections—or at any rate, not with such collections in their original state—that this book is concerned. It is here assumed that, whatever its past history, the present function of the library is to make its collection available to the public, or to a limited or defined section of the public, for the purpose of providing visual documentation in the form of illustrative material, either for study, for research, or for exploitation in some form.

The basic material
That word 'illustration' is so fundamental to the concept of picture librarianship that it is worth giving it some consideration here at the outset of our study. To illustrate means to light up or illumine: the function of most picture libraries is to illumine the minds of those who use them by providing visual information. Each picture has its own piece of information to communicate—what Shakespeare looked like, where Berlin is located in relation to Vienna, how a schooner is rigged, in what form Botticelli visualised the birth of Venus. None of this information could be communicated nearly so effectively, if at all, by verbal description. Each picture in your library contains a scrap, however trivial, of unique information. Some of it will be false information, just as books may contain lies; but even a lie is information.

albeit false information, and though what it tells you about its subject be misleading, what it tells you about its creator, if detected, can be of significance.

Man has stored his scraps of visual information in a bewildering variety of ways. He has painted them on the walls of cave or the sides of jars; he has printed them in popular magazines or photographed them onto cinema film; he has jotted them into private sketchbooks or forced them on the attention of his fellows in the form of political or commercial posters; he has sold them at the scene of executions as broadsheets or sent them through the mail to relatives as postcards; he has given them away in cigarette packets and sold them to wealthy patrons of the arts to ornament their homes; he has printed them privately on hand-made paper to titillate the cupidity of private collectors, and printed them by the million to educate children by means of text-books; he has inscribed them on charts to assist seafarers and printed them in instruction manuals to guide television set repairers; all these, and many more, are pictures, and all may rightfully find their place in a picture library.

Fortunately, in practice, by the time a picture finds its way into a picture library it will have shed its more awkward physical characteristics by being converted to some more practical form. If a cave painting, it will have been photographed; if an oil painting, it may have been engraved; if a poster, it may have been reprinted in reduced format. Though the original may be on canvas, in marble, in tapestry, in coloured lights, by the time it is included in a picture library it is usually in the form of a piece of paper.

For which the picture librarian must be profoundly thankful. Paper is relatively light in weight, and occupies little space. It is remarkably strong and durable, easily stored and easily handled. Compared with the museum curator or the zoo keeper, the picture librarian has a soft job.

There are drawbacks, it is true. Though paper is indeed strong and durable, it is easily damaged or destroyed—it is easily burned, stained, torn, crumpled, stolen. A vandal —or even a careless user—can destroy a Tiepolo drawing or a Byzantine manuscript in less than a second. Paper must be kept at optimum levels of temperature and humidity, and protected from enemies ranging from rusty paperclips to lustful collectors, by way of all kinds of predatory insects and consuming organic growths. And, of course, it is inconsiderate of picture-makers to offer up their work on pieces of paper ranging in size from a postage stamp to a wall-chart —but even this is not so very much worse than the dilemma confronting the book librarian who has to decide whether to put mammoth atlases and pocket gazetteers alongside one another on the bookshelf.

No, the problems facing the picture librarian are all secondary ones. What might have been a serious problem, the diversity of his material, has usually been solved by the time his material reaches him. Perhaps this is the danger: he may be lulled into a sense of false confidence. What major problems can possibly occur, he blithely asks, with a collection of pieces of paper?

His problems start when he asks himself, *why* have those pieces of paper been collected? And *who* have they been collected for?

The function of the picture library
A picture library is a collection of pictures collected for a purpose. That purpose will comprise one, or more often more than one, of the following:

Conservation: It may be felt that if vital or valuable visual documents are to be safely preserved, this will be best done in a collection created for that purpose.

Collection: An individual, or less often an institution, may wish to create a collection of pictures, usually on a particular subject or theme, for its own sake.

Centralisation: It may be felt that there are advantages in gathering visual material relating to a particular subject, for the convenience of those wishing to see, study or use such material. This can be true even when all that is required is to make the pictures available for reference purposes to scholars or other interested persons.

Availability for reproduction: Many picture libraries exist so that publishers, lecturers and the communications media may have convenient access to the material they require.

13

Information: A picture library is *ipso facto* a source of information regarding the pictures in its collection, and perhaps also regarding pictures it does not possess. Many visitors to picture libraries come in search of definitive information about pictures to which they wish to refer in a book, say, or which they plan to reproduce from an un-annotated copy and wish to caption correctly.

Clearly these functions are not mutually exclusive. It will rarely be that a collection is formed only for the sake of the collection itself, though this is certainly an element in the original creation of many collections. Conservation is a motivation in virtually every library, and the advantages of centralisation are self-evident so long as they are not carried to a point where the collection grows too large for practical efficiency. Again, making pictures available for reference is a function of almost every library, while most will add to this the making of them available for exploitation, if only within predetermined limits.

What is important is the degree of emphasis placed upon each of these functions, for it is on this that will depend much of each individual library's policy, whether with regard to acquisition, or devising the organisational structure, or laying down procedural systems and guidelines for access and availability.

Even when the premise is accepted, that a picture collection qualifies as a library only when it makes its material available, on no matter how restricted a level, there is still a wide range of interpretation possible for that word 'available'. There are, for example, those picture collections which may be described—to borrow a useful phrase from another discipline —as 'inner-directed': such might be a collection of Tiepolo drawings, gathered by a connoisseur of Tiepolo drawings who will allow Tiepolo scholars access to the collection to admire and to study. There are, of course, many such collections, mostly in private hands; but even when such collections are bequeathed to public institutions, they hardly constitute picture libraries as we are concerned with them. The curators of such collections will hardly need this book to advise them whether to catalogue their material in chronological or alpha-betical order, to cross index by subject or medium.

14

So we are concerned with picture libraries which may be described as 'outer-directed'. Their purposes may range over as wide a spectrum as human experience and human imagination themselves. At one extreme may be a collection of pictures of insect damage to crops, photographed for a United Nations department; at the other may be a general historical collection, seeking to document the past in every conceivable way. In the following section, a systematic survey of types of picture libraries is made. For the moment, let us simply recognise that this question of purpose cannot be dissociated from the nature of the material on the one hand, and the class of people who will use it on the other. On these will depend the positioning of the picture library on a scale which ranges from the kind that is essentially a collection of pictures *per se*, and that which is essentially a research facility which happens to contain pictures because the subject of research lends itself best to visual documentation.

This is not the place to go deeply into the philosophy of picture collecting. But it is evident that when, say, the British Museum adds to its collection of fifteenth century woodcuts, it does so not, first and foremost, with the interests of the academic thesis writer at heart. Rather, there is felt to be something intrinsically worthwhile in the process of building such a collection, the preservation, collation and cataloguing of such items, so that it becomes almost an end in itself. Carried to its extreme, the process raises the old paradox: is a picture beautiful when nobody is looking at it?, though curators of such collections may reasonably exculpate themselves by pointing out that, by juxtaposing such material, they are facilitating the scholar's task and so making a valid contribution to art scholarship. However, even giving them the benefit of that doubt, it is clear that there is a distinction to be drawn between such a collection and one in which the material is brought together primarily because it is the kind of material which would be useful to those who use the library. In other words, not just 'outer-directed' but 'user-directed'.

But even now we are not through with drawing distinctions. We must still distinguish between the collection whose material defines its usership, and that whose material is

15

defined by its usership. An example of the first would be a collection of visual documents relating to the women's rights movement, which would naturally attract students researching that topic and so define its own public. An example of the second would be the picture library associated with an art college, where the librarian would seek to acquire whatever material would be useful to the students and faculty.

It may seem that these are academic distinctions, unlikely to be of practical concern to the picture librarian, for it is rare that a picture library is created from nothing. When it is, it is almost certainly to serve the needs of a specific institution—a new university, let us say, and this will effectively dictate acquisition policy and access procedure. Nevertheless, the question is not entirely an academic one, for a continued awareness of the function of the library will provide a crucial touchstone when awkward policy decisions need to be made. The librarian of an art reference library intended primarily to serve the day-to-day needs of art students might consider, for instance, that the acquisition of some valuable original material would be inappropriate, since he would be unable to put it safely on open-access along with the main bulk of the collection. On the other hand, he might reflect that perhaps he has a duty to those who use the library to give them the opportunity to examine original material, possessing as it does technical features which are not discernible when the picture is seen in reproduction.

Such questions cannot be answered out of the individual context; there is no correct solution except in terms of the specific library and its role *vis-à-vis* its users. For this reason, the librarian must be clear in his mind what that role is; and this in turn will dictate his priorities. The custodian of a national archive may decide that, however regretfully, he must restrict scholars' access to original material in the interests of conservation; the librarian of a busy reference library may see it as his primary duty to meet the here-and-now needs of his users, and sacrifice longer-term considerations accordingly. There are no absolutes, only variables: to each librarian, his own order of priorities. All that can be said with assurance is that either policy, carried to extremes, will be disastrous, and that an enlightened pragmatism will

16

surely dictate a common-sense answer when dilemmas brandish their horns.

The varieties of picture libraries

One of the most awkward hurdles the picture librarian must jump is a psychological one—he must recognise the fact that picture libraries vary enormously and in every imaginable way. For the term comprehends a range of institutions which comprises at one end of the spectrum the glossy Fleet Street photo agency whose primary function is to supply a visual record of today's news events, world-shattering or trivial, within a few hours of their occurrence; and at the other, the private collection of ephemera which a dedicated enthusiast diffidently makes available to those who seek him out where he sits like a miser with his hoard. Picture libraries vary in size, in scope and in function, as well as in countless lesser ways such as their degree of helpfulness to the public and readiness to facilitate exploitation. The categories described here represent only those most frequently encountered.

Public collections, general

Most public collections such as the British Museum, the British Library, the Victoria and Albert Museum, and their equivalents in other countries, have picture libraries of their own. These may be limited to making available photographs or reproductions of items within their own primary collections, or may possess supplementary material. Thus the National Portrait Gallery has a substantial picture collection, containing prints and engravings of intrinsic value and also cuttings from newspapers and magazines filed for reference purposes, backing up its primary collection. Clearly, the question of conservation is of primary importance here; and next, the making available of the material to scholars. Exploitation comes way down the list, as is evidenced by the lengthy delays in supplying copies of their material which are encountered in the majority of such institutions.

Public archives, specific

Many government departments, such as the Foreign and

Commonwealth Offices, maintain their own picture archives. Access to these is generally limited to approved researchers who can show that no other source will meet their needs. Here again, conservation heads the list of priorities, and though the staff at an institution such as the Public Records Office will do their best to assist the user, the material is not organised with exploitation as a primary consideration.

Public archives, regional & local
Institutions such as the Greater London Council have their own picture collections—in this instance, two collections, one of maps, prints and drawings, the other of photographs. Other institutions have associated collections which are recognised repositories of relevant material, as the Guildhall acts in regard to the City of London, housing much material concerning the City, its guilds and other institutions. As a consequence, the material in such collections is apt to comprise a somewhat haphazard-seeming assortment of individual bequests and acquisitions, donated or purchased sporadically, and perhaps in accordance with the fluctuating policies laid down by succeeding generations of curators. Nevertheless enlightened 'gap-filling' can often ensure that the end-result is a wide-ranging and balanced collection which, though not 'user-directed' as we have defined the term, can be a veritable treasure-house for the researcher.

Societies
Specialised institutions, such as the Royal Geographical Society, frequently possess important collections of material, originally created for the use of members. Where, as in this instance, it is evident that the collection is of unique public importance, access is generally allowed to outsiders, when sufficient cause can be shown and within specified limitations.

Professional bodies
Institutions such as the Royal Institute of British Architects often maintain their own on-going collections for the convenience of their members. Though primarily intended as reference sources for those actively engaged in that particular profession, it is recognised that they have an additional value

18

as research facilities for outsiders, and most public-spirited organisations will grant access in the same way as the societies referred to above.

Commercial and industrial firms

Certain industries are catered for by specialist libraries. Perhaps the best-known example is the St Bride Printing Library, which is, in fact, a public library located just off Fleet Street and created as a reference source for all concerned with printing and related activities. The nature of this particular industry makes it a 'natural' for such a collection, but it is surprising that not more individual trades have set up such reference sources to meet their own needs. Perhaps the explanation is to be found in competition within the industry? Fortunately, many individual firms maintain reference collections, usually in association with their press or public relations departments. In some cases—Shell, Dunlop and Sainsbury's are examples—these have built up over the years into substantial collections, ranging over a considerably wider field than the day-to-day activities of the firm in question. In the case of Shell, for example, the picture library is an important source of material relating to ecology and agricultural development, especially in underdeveloped areas. Such material is generally made available to the public on prescribed conditions.

A more recent development in this field is the industrial museum, which usually takes the form of an industrial building restored to something like its original state and provided with artifacts illustrating the processes involved. Clearly, visual documentation is essential for such enterprises, and the better organised museums have formed associated picture collections which are made available to the public. Similarly, collections such as the National Motor Museum at Beaulieu have extremely valuable specialist picture collections.

Press agencies

Every country in the world possesses a number of firms whose business it is to gather news photographs from their own country and make them available internationally, and likewise to gather such material from abroad and make it available in their own country. Inevitably, this is an exceedingly hectic business, since pictures must be made available in a matter of hours on the far side of the globe, and copies made available for immediate use by newspapers and other media. The great majority of such pictures lose their value within a few hours of their creation, but they are generally held for a given period. It is usual to maintain back files, though their degree of organisation and standards of availability vary enormously. In some cases the older material is administered separately—even by a completely independent organisation—at which stage they become picture libraries in their own right, qualifying as historical archives rather than news agencies.

Photo agencies
Probably the largest single category of picture libraries consists of agencies which handle the work of photographers who deal in non-topical material, ranging from scenes and views of all parts of the world to photographs of wildlife, scientific subjects, transport and every kind of specialist interest. Some of these agencies are general in scope, enormous libraries containing millions of pictures on almost every imaginable subject and catering for every kind of user from book publishers to greetings card manufacturers and calendar designers. Others are more or less specialised, representing particular interests such as horticulture or steam engines, industrial archeology or space exploration.

Except for those maintained by government departments or tourist offices, which have clearly defined exploitation or propaganda functions, photo agencies are invariably commercial in character, dependent on the revenue derived from the use of their material. Here, availability is the first priority, and a high degree of organisation is a prerequisite for success.

Historical reference archives
Sharing to some degree the characteristics of both the public collection and the commercial agency, are those picture libraries which contain only historical material, but which are geared primarily to exploitation by their users, this providing

20

their sole source of revenue. To a large extent, such collections duplicate the kind of material that is found in public archives, but with the difference that, being wholly dependent on their users for survival, they are likely to respond more flexibly to those users' needs. While such collections generally have sufficient social conscience to take due care to conserve their material, their first obligation has to be to provide an effective service to their users. This necessitates a high degree of organisation and the provision of the facilities necessary for maximum convenience of research and opportunity for exploitation.

Summary
Such are the main categories of picture libraries existing today. In practice, the lines of demarcation between them may not be as sharp as the description suggests, nor does it follow that any two picture libraries which happen to be in the same category will necessarily resemble each other. Even when the subject-matter is the same and the usership similar, there is room for wide variations in practice, and it can happen that a picture library will more closely resemble another in quite a different category than one which in principle it should exactly duplicate!

This is to be seen most evidently in regard to what might seem to be the most clear-cut dividing line of all—that which separates the commercial from the non-commercial collections. Though the fact of being wholly dependent for its revenue on the exploitation of its material might seem to be crucial in determining the character of a library, in practice the distinction turns out to be more apparent than real. Every picture library has to obtain an income from somewhere, and whether it comes in the form of a direct subsidy, or as income derived from exploitation, need not make so great a difference. Someone, after all, is paying in every case: in the case of public institutions, art colleges and so forth, it is the taxpayer or the rates payer; whereas in the case of commercial libraries it is the user himself.

Again, what is one to say of a firm like the Shell Picture Library already mentioned, which will generally make its material available free of charge? Strictly speaking, that makes it non-commercial; whereas it is evident that though Shell may indeed provide such material as a public service, it does so largely to enhance its good name and is rewarded in credit if not in cash. Similarly, most ministries of tourism maintain picture libraries which will lend material without charge. Here again, though technically non-commercial, the purpose is certainly gain of a kind.

The moral is, in short, that even sticking a label on his collection does not excuse the picture librarian from the agonising process of decision making. It is still up to him, within a wide range of manoeuvre, to determine the lines of policy and procedure appropriate to the role his library performs and the public it serves. How he carries out every process and operation described in the remainder of this book will be affected by how he answers the questions *why, and for whom, his library exists*. And those are two questions this book cannot answer for him.

TWO

ACQUISITION

The starting point
Lucky the librarian who starts with an empty room. He can lay down principles of acquisition from the beginning, and ensure that all material is acquired along those principles, accepting or rejecting as his chosen guidelines dictate, building into a coherent and homogeneous whole. . .

In practice this never happens. Even the librarian of a brand-new university, entrusted with the delightful task of building up a picture library from scratch, is liable to have legacies or donations given him which will contain material he would not, of his own will, have chosen to acquire. Or he will purchase an existing collection as his nucleus, and be forced to accept extraneous material along with what he truly wants. All picture libraries are made up in varying proportions of material deliberately acquired—and thus conforming more or less to some ideal blueprint—and material accidentally obtained, which may well be far from ideal. And even this does not take into account fluctuations of policy, as librarian succeeds librarian and brings—as he is sure to bring, if he is a true and creative librarian, not merely a custodian—his own values and guidelines.

Consequently, most picture librarians will find themselves in the position of having to administer a 'given' collection bequeathed to them from the past, and only imperfectly suited to the library's functions in the present. Sometimes there will be gaps, sometimes there will be disproportions and imbalances, sometimes there will be, hardly less embarrassingly, bulges.

What he does about this will probably depend on his temperament. To use Koestler's archetypes: if he is a

Commissar he will ruthlessly prune the collection until he is left only with what conforms to the 'party-line', whereas if he is a Yogi he will philosophically accept things as he finds them and seek to make the best of the serendipitous situation, gaps and bulges and all. Once again, the role and usership of the individual library is likely to encourage one attitude rather than the other; an efficiency-conscious commercial agency is more likely to be embarrassed by extraneous material than a public library. But whether it retains or discards, each should be continually striving to mould its collection into a coherent whole and ironing out any unevenness.

Gaps and bulges
The gaps are the simplest to deal with. Note should be taken of items or subjects which are requested by users of the library which the library is unable to provide, and a list of desiderata built up, to which those members of the staff concerned with acquisition can continually refer.

In practice, it is not long before staff become acutely aware of the collection's more obvious lacks, and will be on a constant watch for pictures of the Tolpuddle Martyrs, or a portrait of Marlowe, or a representation of a man walking in front of a motor car with a red flag—to name three elusive items notorious to any historical picture librarian! There will also be subject areas in which the library is particularly weak, so that staff are on a permanent look out for additional material to supplement their industrial material, say, or Russian art. It is a good idea to have a 'WANTED' notice up on the staff notice board, on which the more notable gaps are listed, to be crossed off—hopefully—as and when they are supplied.

Another helpful practice can be to maintain a Visitors' Book in which users state the object of their visit to the library. From this it is possible to make a periodic assessment of the range of motives which bring users to the library, and this may in turn suggest areas where the material or the service might, if feasible, be strengthened. In addition, such information provides useful 'hard' support for any application for funds for adding to the collection.

When the converse is true, and the library finds itself with a superfluity of a certain category of material, the matter must be considered on practical grounds. If, for instance, some kind person has donated to the library a collection of material which is extraneous to the general subject-matter, the librarian must consider whether to refuse the gift or re-direct it in a more appropriate direction, or somehow to keep it as a special collection.

Where the subject is not too incompatible, the decision is more likely to be in favour of keeping it—librarians are for the most part acquisitive by nature, prone more to retain than to discard. Thus we find Bromley Public Library with a special collection of material relating to the Crystal Palace, which is located not too far away geographically, and Mary Evans Picture Library with a collection of Sigmund Freud family photographs which are not inconsistent with that library's general policy of visual documentation of the past. Thus in both cases 'bulges' can be seen as acceptable even though they do represent an imbalance.

It is not so easy to know what to do when the material is not closely relevant. For example, the Guildhall Library possesses a collection of superb old master prints, which do not, on the face of it, seem to have very much to do with the library's primary collection of material relating to the history of London. Some might argue that in such cases a librarian will do best to dispose of the material, and use the money to purchase additional material more directly related to his specific field; others would prefer to retain the material, even though perhaps most users of the library do not even know that it is there, simply because having got hold of it they may as well hang on to it, and in time ways of using it may be found.

Often, of course, the librarian has no option, as when the material is in the form of a bequest, perhaps accepted by a former librarian, which cannot now be alienated from the rest of the collection. In such a case he has little choice but to live with it as best he can—or, of course, pack it away in crates and leave it in the basement.

Between the gaps and the bulges are the imbalances, causing a library to find itself with a distinct bias towards a certain type of material. For instance, of two collections of photographs from India, one may find itself with material depicting everyday life and working conditions, while the other may consist entirely of architectural monuments or political events. In such cases the librarian has to make the decision whether to try to compensate for the bias by subsequent acquisition, or make a virtue of it by drawing users' attention to the type of item in which the collection is particularly strong.

Probably the deciding factor in such a case will be determined by the kind of user the library caters for; but in general it can be said that it is not necessarily a bad thing for a library to be known as particularly useful for a certain type of material. Such a reputation gives the library a recognisable 'character', and can in fact act as a lure to attract users who will then discover what else the collection has to offer. The danger, of course, is that the collection will become typecast, like an actor known for playing heavy fathers—'they only have Victorian engravings' when this is only one facet of the collection. But this in turn can be countered by judicious public relations—for instance, by mounting an in-house exhibition of material diametrically opposed to that for which the collection is chiefly known—photographs from the twenties if it is known for its Victorian engravings, fashion plates if it is noted for its old steam engines.

The ideal collection
Whether he starts with an empty room or with stacks of cardboard boxes and brown paper parcels full of pictures which have been donated, or with an on-going collection with its share of gaps and bulges, the librarian should nevertheless form and keep in his mind's eye an ideal collection—a Platonic ideal of the library as he would wish it to be. No matter that the actual library will never be better than a short-falling approximation to that ideal. To see continually before him a dream library in which all gaps shall be filled, all bulges smoothed out, will give him the vital guidelines he will need when considering the acquisition of additional material.

Over-riding all guidelines is this general rule, to which his acquisitive instinct should make it easy for him to conform: when in doubt, say 'Yes'. It is a matter of every collector's experience that you regret far more the items you should have acquired, but did not, than the things you should not have acquired, but did.

Nevertheless, there are such things as budgets, and space restrictions; and these will curb the impulse to acquire and compel the librarian to restrain his instincts. It is at this stage that various criteria come into play to define the limits of that ideal library:

range of subject matter
compatibility of subject matter
relevance to the function of the library
considerations of size.

In practice these factors are all inter-dependent, and will not exert their force in isolation. But some observations on each may be helpful.

Range of subject matter
The broad outlines of subject matter will have been determined when the library was created, and will be geared to the needs of those who use the library. However, it is unlikely that they will have been precisely formulated, and account should be taken of changing needs; so each librarian, on assuming office, should re-consider the matter in the light of circumstances as they now exist. Thus a picture library specialising in architectural subjects will be affected by the contemporary trend towards conservation, while one which is concerned with agriculture or land use will recognise the current concern for environment and ecology.

Then, when the general direction of the collection is firmly set, there will be the secondary decisions. If the collection is a historical one, is the cut-off date to be a fixed one—1914 or 1939, say, or is it to be steadily advanced as time itself advances—marching, perhaps, a steady twenty five years behind the true date, on the grounds that today's actuality is tomorrow's history? If the collection is one of portraits of personalities, will this be extended to include pictures of their birthplaces and homes, title pages of their books and records of their achievements? If it is a scientific collection, is it to include fringe subjects such as UFOs and acupuncture, parapsychology and alchemy? In short, round the boundaries of every subject there lie marginal areas which may be included or excluded, as the librarian decides.

Compatibility
There is a certain picture library in London where they have a brown paper parcel containing a collection of promotional items emanating from a now defunct department store. Such material is now recognised as uniquely valuable, and the library is well aware of the fact; at the same time, the material is not really compatible with the rest of their material and is consequently something of an embarrassment.

Almost every librarian is plagued by awkward little problems of this sort, for even though he may not maintain an active acquisition policy, he is liable to have such items wished on him by well-meaning donors who are themselves perhaps embarrassed by the material and anxious only that it should find, somewhere, 'a good home'. Rather than condemn himself to a continual series of one-off decisions, the librarian will be well advised to make a once-for-all policy formulation, whether to adhere strictly to a predetermined blueprint and reject any extraneous item on principle, or to accept and add whatever comes his way regardless of its relevance, or to seek a compromise by establishing a 'thus far and no farther' line which will permit certain categories to be retained but require others to be passed on to some more suitable place. Thus one picture library accepts any material in any way relevant to social history, but firmly rejects any material relating to the fine arts, no matter how attractive, because there is simply no way in which it can be integrated with the rest of the collection.

A picture is of value to a collection only when there is a reasonable expectation that someone will expect to find it there, and this provides a convenient touchstone for decision making. If the librarian is forced to admit that none of his habitual users would expect to find such material in his collection, then he will do better to hand it over to a more appropriate collection. This is not only in the user's interest, it also makes things easier for his own staff, who will not be required to remember that the collection includes that particular anomaly, giving it attention out of all proportion to its usefulness.

Relevance to the function of the library
Material may fall within the subject limits of the collection, and yet be inappropriate to the practical requirements of the library. For example, a library which caters to the needs of art students may have the opportunity to acquire a collection of old master etchings. At first sight, the librarian is likely to be attracted by the thought of adding such material; but he may then reflect that the real need of those who use the library is for transparency reproductions of pictures, which they can borrow and use as they wish, and that original material of this nature, however intrinsically desirable, does not really belong in a reference library. If it is offered as a free gift, of course, he will probably accommodate it, justifying the decision on the grounds that it is no bad thing to have some original material to back up the copy collection; but if it is a question of purchase, he may well decide, reluctantly, that the money could be more usefully spent.

Considerations of size
Finally, while a librarian should always be thinking in terms of growth, he must recognise that size has its drawbacks. Every item added places an additional burden on his staff: it must be catalogued, filed, indexed, cross-referenced and so forth. So it must justify all that work, as well as the space it will occupy.

Similarly, there may be too much material from some users' point of view. An example might be the John Johnson collection of ephemera at the Bodleian Library, Oxford. While nobody is suggesting that they should get rid of half their collection, the fact is that there is such a wealth of material that the researcher, unless he is very clear in his mind about what precisely he is looking for, is liable to be overwhelmed by such an *embarras de richesse*.

What can a librarian do in such a case? He can be selective, perhaps keeping some of the less useful material in a store room; but to do that he will need to be very sure of what is useful and what is not, and certainly must make sure that the stored material is reasonably accessible and properly cared for and catalogued. But such considerations provide a guide-line in the matter of acquisition, where he should ask himself, even when offered material which falls within the scope of his collection, whether it truly justifies the work and space it will demand.

A librarian would be less than human if, after formulating his own guidelines, he never allowed himself to trespass beyond them from time to time. Indeed, such trespassing is wholly to be desired, for it is likely that some deeper instinct —that flair which every creative librarian should possess—is guiding him in making a decision which runs counter to his own rule.

Breaking a rule does not invalidate it. It is still desirable for the librarian, faced with the opportunity to acquire additional material, to ask himself: Does it fall within the scope of our subject matter? Is it compatible with what we already possess? Will it be genuinely useful to those who use the library? Does it add enough to the collection to justify the work it will require and the space it will occupy? He may indeed answer 'No' to all four, and nevertheless decide to go ahead and acquire it—but at least he will do so in the full knowledge of what his decision entails.

How a picture library is built up
Pictures come into a picture library in many different ways; the principal ones are detailed below.

Initial foundation
Most picture collections are given some kind of a start in life, with an existing collection as a nucleus, bequeathed or donated or purchased: it could take the form of a dedicated collector's private hoard, or a photographer's past files. Sometimes the collection is never added to—it remains static, a collection of Rembrandt etchings or suchlike, whose librarian has only a curator's functions, not being called upon to formulate an acquisition policy because the question does not arise. Such cases are rare, however: even such specialised collections are generally concerned to fill gaps or add complementary material.

Regular intake
Certain types of picture libraries are by their very nature the recipients of an on-going supply of fresh material. The most

30

obvious example is the news agency, which every day receives a supply of photographs chronicling the day's events. Many photo agencies, likewise, are based on the work of a photographer or team of photographers, with fresh instalments continually adding to the stock after each assignment.

Sporadic continual acquisition
Some picture libraries are built up from material obtained in irregular batches. An example would be a picture library associated with a publisher where every time a book is published, material made or collected for that book would be filed in the picture library for possible future use.

Gifts
Certain types of picture libraries, particularly public institutions, tend to be recipients of donations of various kinds. A local historian, who has gathered material to help him in his work, is likely to leave it to the local public library as the most suitable repository, preferring that it should be maintained as a collection rather than dispersed. Clearly it is in the interests of such collections, if they welcome acquisitions of this sort, to make discreet advances if they know of particular potential donors, or at least to let it be generally known that they welcome such gifts. Sometimes the gifts come with strings attached—it may be stipulated that the collection be kept as an autonomous whole, and perhaps even designated as the 'John Smith Memorial Library' or whatever, but if the material is sufficiently desirable, the library will accept this. Most often, though, it is likely to be a case of a widow wanting to get rid of her husband's old papers, and only too happy to find a good home for them.

Acquisition of complete collections
Occasionally the opportunity will arise for the library to acquire a complete collection at once. A typical example would be a collector who has devoted a large part of his life to building up a collection, and who might be glad to know that it will survive him. A tactful approach, pointing out that its chances of survival will be very much greater if entrusted

to an established picture library, may well secure the collection at a price well below that which it might obtain in the open market, or even as an outright gift.

Another opportunity for such acquisitions is provided by commercial firms, professional societies and the like, who may possess picture archives which are something of an embarrassment to them. In such a case the collection itself may be entrusted to the library as a permanent loan on given terms. There are many examples of this in British public libraries.

An alternative procedure is for the picture library to offer to copy the archive, and so, while leaving the original material with the owner, to make copies available to a wider public. This is particularly suitable for private institutions, such as learned societies or professional bodies, who may possess valuable archives which they know to be of interest to outsiders, but which they are not equipped to make available to the public simply because they lack the facilities. In such a case the picture library can handle all the administrative side and the society can refer inquirers to the library, saving itself a great deal of inconvenience and also safeguarding its material from much wear and tear.

On-going purchase programme
But for most picture libraries the method of acquisition is likely to be a continuous process of purchase, usually of single items or small batches. It is with this that we shall be concerned throughout the remainder of this chapter.

Given unlimited funds, such a policy is not too difficult to implement. The librarian would simply have to define the scope of the collection, identify gaps or weak areas, and then set about the joyous task of filling them by every possible means available. However, the librarian who has access to unlimited funds has probably never existed, not even in a well-endowed American university in the heyday of dollar prosperity, so that acquisition becomes yet another area for continual decision making.

To finance his purchase programme, the librarian will normally have access either to a purchase fund, or to a budget allowed to him by the owners of the library. In either case, this is likely to be seen by him as an allowance that he can spend, usually on an annual basis; though if he is fortunate he will know that, should an exceptional opportunity arise, he will receive a sympathetic hearing if he asks for a supplementary budget. In any case, it is as well to make it clear to anyone who holds the purse strings that the acquisition of pictures cannot be compared with any of the other overheads of the establishment, like ordering stationery or equipment. For the most part, you do not go out and buy pictures the way you buy typewriters or index files; it is a matter of seizing opportunities, which may arise erratically and unexpectedly.

Consequently, though the cost of purchases will even out in the long term, at the time they will cause unpredictable fluctuations in the account book. To budget for time-spans of less than a year would be unrealistic. Furthermore, the opportunity must be seized immediately, before someone else gets it: consequently the purchase money likewise must be immediately and constantly available, and the librarian granted complete authority to conclude purchases without reference to any other individual or body.

And so, by hook or by crook, the librarian obtains his budget, and receives authority to use it as he sees fit within the stipulated guidelines he has been given. Now it is up to him to see what he can do to transform the real-life library he administers into as close a replica as he can manage of that 'ideal library' he carries in his head.

Sources of material
Leaving aside on-going additions from artists, photographers and other regular sources, and donations over which he has no control, where is the librarian to look for material to fill his gaps and build up his weak areas? The answer will, of course, depend in part on the size of budget he is allowed; but other factors will also play a part. Here are some of the possibilities.

Sales and auctions
On the face of it, these seem the most likely source for acquiring material. Any item of real value, if it appears in the public market at all, is likely to do so at a sale or auction;

this is particularly true when collections are being broken up, or when collectors are disposing of items they no longer wish to keep. For any librarian who is on the higher levels of picture acquisition, subscription to the catalogues of all major auction houses will be an essential investment, and it will be a regular part of his duties to go through those catalogues, visit the salerooms to view the material, and either attend the sales or commission agents to bid on behalf of the library.

At the same time, it should be recognised that buying at sales has several drawbacks, particularly for libraries whose budgets fall short of what the librarian would consider a realistic figure. Prices at sales, particularly the big and well-publicised sales where the finest material is up for auction, are at the highest rates going—indeed, it is often at such sales that new record prices are established. And so while bargains continue to occur, in these days when material is becoming less and less available, and when collectors are growing more knowledgeable and more keen to invest their money in such an attractive way, the chances of acquiring worthwhile items at below-value prices are few and far between

Local sales are a different matter—but then few libraries can afford the time required to visit such events on the off-chance that they will have anything worth having. It will probably work out cheaper to buy from the dealers who can afford to invest their time in that way.

So, though the sales room should not be wholly ignored, it should be visited only sparingly, when an item crops up which is going to be of real value to the library; and for that, the librarian should be prepared to pay over the odds, if necessary. For the emotional climate of the sales room plays its part in sending up prices, and however cool-headed the librarian himself may be, he will be competing against dedicated collectors who are motivated by fierce passions transcending everyday sense.

Shops and markets
It is likely that the librarian will forge regular relationships with certain shops which tend to deal in the kind of material he requires. Today there are few print shops in Britain

compared with the number half a century ago, but this is largely made up for by the proliferation of antique dealers, many of whom offer engravings and similar items for sale. Some will have a reasonably rapid turn-round of stock, so that a visit every month or so is worthwhile; to others, a visit once a year will be sufficient. Once he has formed a steady relationship with such a shop, of course, the librarian can leave a wants list with them, or give them some indication as to the sort of material in which he is likely to be interested, so they will let him know if something in his line should come their way.

Prices in shops tend to be more realistic than in the sales room, and though their prices are in turn affected by those established at auctions, there will always be a time lag before prices catch up with the newly fixed high.

By and large—and this is liable to surprise the newcomer to picture buying—the best prices are often to be obtained at the largest and most knowledgeable establishments. Small dealers, especially those for whom pictures are only a sideline, are apt to suppose that any print more than a hundred years old must automatically be worth a substantial sum of money, whereas the experienced print dealer knows that the value of apparently comparable prints can be very different, and furthermore that price does not go hand in hand with age. Small local antique shops may indeed contain splendid bargains, but they are also likely to contain pictures at absurdly inflated prices.

No shop is too humble for the librarian to visit. One leading historical collection recently acquired a very fine print of the execution of Charles I for 20 pence in the 'throw-out' box on the pavement outside a print shop. Flea markets are a useful as well as a pleasant source of material: the same collection found some of De Brij's prints of the Spanish conquistadores, from the late sixteenth century, for 50 pence a piece in the Marché aux Puces in Paris.

Postal dealers

For many picture librarians the most useful sources are the one-man businesses which operate by circulating their catalogues, usually once a month, listing material which can be

35

ordered from them. These dealers, who spend their lives going round shops and sale rooms, act as valuable middlemen who can save the librarian a great deal of hunting. Here again, it is usually possible to establish a good working relationship so that they can be on the lookout for the type of material in which a particular library is interested.

Dealing with such vendors can be a nerve-wracking business. So great is the demand nowadays, that it is usually necessary to read through their catalogues immediately upon receiving them, and phone through orders without a moment's delay. The librarian of Winchester College a few years ago was chagrined when early one morning he phoned a dealer for a run of *Punch* listed in his latest catalogue, only to find that he had been beaten to the post by another picture librarian who had phoned before breakfast and got the dealer out of bed! This is a ruthless field to work in, and it calls for ruthless decision-making.

Many of these dealers will take back material which, on receipt, the buyer does not want; for, though many of the items can be identified by verbal description, obviously the drawback of this method of buying is that the purchaser does not see what he is buying. Others will send out material on approval, though usually only when no other customer has placed a firm order.

Naturally, the prices charged by dealers of this kind are higher than you would have paid had you been to the shop or the sale yourself. But in practice, the time and expense you would have incurred would probably cancel out the money you might have saved.

Casual offerings

It may happen that the library will get visitors coming in off the street, with a couple of items in a plastic bag. Surprisingly, such visits can often be rewarding. For every one who comes in with some worthless souvenir book, there is likely to be one who comes in with something interesting—some old postcards found in a shoe box on a cupboard shelf, some old family photos from the loft. Only recently an elderly lady came wandering in to one London picture library and produced from her handbag signed photographs of Victoria and

George V, together with some water colours by two of Victoria's children, for which she wanted only a very reasonable £25. So the moral is, never turn away such visitors, however unpromising, without at least taking a look at what they are offering.

Perhaps all this sounds very hit-and-miss, but that is just what the picture market is. Unlike shirts or cheese, pictures are not things you can simply go out and purchase when you feel the need; just because you have a gap in your collection does not mean that you have only to go out, money in hand, to fill it. Pictures have to be hunted for, watched and waited for, and the chance taken promptly and decisively when it occurs. The watchword of the librarian must be eternal vigilance. He must keep his eyes open wherever he goes, on work or on holiday; in foreign cities he must visit the flea markets, his Saturday afternoons must be spent haunting suburban booksellers and jumble sales.

A postscript on prices
Often the librarian will have to make up his own mind whether a picture is worth the price that is being asked; sometimes he will actually have to name a price. How do you estimate the value of a couple of folders, containing negatives and prints relating to the Women's Suffrage movement, about 125 items, some of them genuine old photographs, some copied from periodicals. . . The answer is, over the years you develop a sort of flair. In this true instance, it subsequently turned out that the vendor had the figure £300 in mind, while the library was prepared to—and did—offer £350. How either party had arrived at their selected figure they would probably have found it impossible to say, and perhaps each started by wondering as what point between £50—which must be too little—and £1000—obviously too much—was the proper figure. The fact that both came to much the same figure indicates that, arbitrary as it may seem, there is some kind of intuition which confirms the rule-of-thumb estimate.

When the market price of an item is fixed, things are of course easier; it then becomes simply a question of deciding whether you are willing to pay that price or not. But, even here, the question can be usefully rephrased. It should not be, Is this picture worth this price? but, Is it worth this price to *me*?

For example, suppose the going price of a single volume of a long-running periodical is £25, and suppose you see a volume offered for £40, your first instinct might be not to pay a price which is clearly well over the odds. But then, suppose that happens to be the one volume which is needed to make up your set, which would have the effect of adding substantially to the value of the entire run? In such a case it would be well worth paying the asked price, outrageously high though it may be.

More often, though, one rebels—and rightly—against paying over the odds. An extremely wealthy French singer was quoted recently in the press: when asked why he had not purchased a particular item it was known he wished to add to his collection, he explained that though the price was not too high for *him*, it was too high for that item.

This principle, of evaluating the article on the basis of what it is worth to you rather than what it might be worth on the open market, can be of particular usefulness when someone comes to the library with a picture or collection of pictures and asks you to make an offer for it. It saves a deal of embarrassment if you can say to him, 'My offer is not intended as an estimate of what your goods may be worth to others, I can only tell you what they are worth to this library.' You may then make an offer which otherwise he might have considered insultingly low, but which he is compelled to respect when presented on those terms.

THREE

CARE AND MAINTENANCE

WHETHER he sees himself primarily as the custodian of valuable material, or simply as the provider of a useful service, the picture librarian must take care of his pictures. Certain procedures will vary according to the purpose to which the pictures are to be put, but the basic principle—that the pictures should be preserved in optimum condition—remains the same.

General considerations
A word of caution is perhaps appropriate here. To preserve pictures in optimum condition sounds to us like a reasonable ideal, for we live in an age of conservationism where anything and everything is regarded as worth caring for. Certainly, if the pendulum has to swing in one direction rather than another, this is a healthy extreme—better that too much should be retained than too little; and in the aftermath of two world wars in which so much priceless material was destroyed for ever, we should certainly seek to reduce further losses as best we can. But that is not the same as saying that *everything* is worth any amount of trouble to preserve. Since the beginning of the nineteenth century we have lived in a world where mass communication through the printed word has resulted in an ever-increasing quantity of books being produced. It stands to reason that a great deal of them are worthless, or only of temporary worth until a better book should replace them.

This is not an argument for wholesale destruction, but simply a caveat against misplaced reverence. The picture librarian must keep his head in this respect. A certain London photo agency recently asked an experienced editor to go through its material, weeding out the items which were simply not worth keeping in the files. She was able to eliminate some twenty-five per cent of the pictures, all of which were—by any normal standard—excellent pictures; but which she knew. from her professional experience, would never be used by a picture editor, because they would not reproduce satisfactorily, or because their 'message' was confused, or because better pictures on the same subject were available.

Clearly that is an extreme case, but it does highlight the probability that in any collection of pictures there is likely to be a proportion of material which is simply not worth preserving—not worth the staff time spent on it, the work of cleaning, cataloguing, captioning and filing, or even the space it occupies.

No guidelines can be laid down in this respect, for only the particular circumstances in which a library's material is used will reveal which items are valuable, which are useless. All that can be done here is to recommend keeping a sense of proportion, so that valuable time and space is not wasted on material which does not warrant it.

The care of photographs, negatives and transparencies

A great many picture libraries consist solely of photographic items—black and white prints and their negatives, or colour transparencies of various sizes. Indeed, there are many picture libraries which contain nothing but 35mm transparencies, which means that enormous numbers of pictures can be easily kept in a very small space. But even when the material is more disparate, photographs are relatively easy to look after. At the same time it must be remembered that photographic items are more sensitive than printed items, simply because they are created by chemical means related to certain substances' sensitivity to light. However effectively 'fixed', no photograph can be regarded as absolutely permanent. The well-known fading of photographs from the nineteenth century, giving that pale sepia effect so familiar and so nostalgic, is just one of the many things that can happen to a photograph simply with the passage of time.

40

Since then, of course, there have been technical developments which diminish the danger of deterioration, while storage techniques have also been developed which make preservation more controllable. And there is always the cheering thought that if a copyprint should deteriorate, it can always be replaced simply by running off another from the negative if it exists.

Nonetheless, it is obviously desirable to give copyprints a reasonable degree of care. Obviously they should not be folded in two, bent or creased or scratched. They should be stored in such a way that they are flat, whether upright or horizontal; they should not be exposed to light, especially sunlight, for longer than is necessary, and handling should be kept to a minimum. As to how they should best be stored, this will depend on the procedure of the individual library, and will be discussed in the following chapter.

Up to a point, the black and white copyprint can be regarded as an expendable item. A reasonable degree of care will ensure that it does not have to be replaced too frequently, but beyond that there is no point in expending more than a minimum of care on it.

With the original negative, on the other hand, it is of course a very different matter. Photographic negatives are long-lived if well cared for, but very vulnerable to damage and deterioration. They should be stored individually, never in contact with other negatives, in plastic or paper envelopes or wallets; they should be kept out of the light and exposed to it only when necessary; and they should be kept at normal levels of humidity and temperature, the actual level not being particularly crucial, but avoiding extreme fluctuations. Most importantly, negatives should be handled as little as possible; they should, therefore, be kept in see-through containers of some kind, so that inspection can be carried out without removing them from the container. The chemical effect of a fingerprint on a negative can do more lasting damage than almost any other form of ill-treatment.

What is true of negatives is generally true of transparencies, but here the librarian has a more serious problem. For while negatives can be kept shut away, to be removed from the file only when necessary for checking or for obtaining additional prints, transparencies are intended for daily use, and constant handling is unavoidable.

First and foremost, therefore, transparencies must be housed in containers to eliminate actual contact, whether of human hand, or dust or any other material object which could stain, scratch or mark them. Ideally, a see-through plastic container will be used, and ideally a separate wallet for each transparency. This can of course be expensive, and it is general practice, especially with the standard 35mm transparency size, to house them in sets of twenty-four in suspended plastic files. This means that they have to be removed whenever they are needed, though fortunately not when they are simply being inspected; and so there is an inevitable degree of dangerous handling, which need not be serious if those who do the handling are professionals, but which lays the item open to mishandling from the inexpert and the ignorant. The librarian who has to cater for the latter, therefore, should see to it that all who use or borrow his transparencies receive basic instruction in the do's and don't's of handling such vulnerable items.

With transparencies as with negatives, it is important not to expose them to extremes of heat or cold, or to severe fluctuations of humidity. They should not be left in the open, and especially in light boxes or tables, for longer than is necessary, nor left where they can attract dust—to which, being plastic, they are very liable.

Here again, the actual form of storage will depend on access procedures, to be discussed in the following chapter.

The care of prints and engravings
When an engraving is purchased at a high class auction, or from a dealer of repute, the chances are that it will already be clean, in good repair and securely mounted. But this will not apply to many items acquired more casually—for example, to prints found in an antique shop or on a market stall. Such pictures may require a good deal of physical attention before they are ready for incorporation into the files of the library.

In the first place, they may require cleaning. Many old prints are stained, or foxed, or coated with dust, or simply

42

yellowed with time and poor storage. Only too often there are water marks showing where damp has crept into the box or portfolio where the prints may have been undisturbed for years. Fortunately, most such damage is not lasting; paper, for all its fragility, is an astonishingly durable and resilient material—it can be wetted and dried time and time again with very little loss of quality, and many of the more serious stains can be easily removed.

All such defects should, of course, be attended to as soon as the picture is acquired; not because they themselves require urgent treatment, but because it should be a fundamental principle of the library not to keep any items on the premises which are not in good state and ready for immediate use.

The actual steps to be taken will vary according to the nature of the damage and the value of the original. If it is an item of real worth, then expert advice should be taken. A picture library which habitually acquires valuable material will either have an expert on its staff, or will have a standing arrangement with an outside expert to whom all such items are regularly passed. Sometimes an item will be so fragile that it is best to do nothing at all; but restoration techniques are now so sophisticated that it is rare that nothing can be done.

For less valuable items, where less is at stake, the library should possess its own facilities for cleaning and making minor repairs. Most old prints can be easily relieved of their minor blemishes by being bathed for a while in a solution of bleach—the ordinary household variety; this will remove foxing and many other stains, water and damp mould, and restore the whiteness of the paper where the picture has turned yellow with the years. This applies noticeably to cheap newsprint, such as that used for the illustrated periodicals of the nineteenth century. Pictures from these periodicals can be greatly enhanced by leaving them for an hour or so—the actual time duration is not critical—in a bath of dilute bleach, after which the paper will be white and the picture image crisper and more contrasty. Certain marks, however, notably those caused by rusty paper clips, are almost impossible to remove; all that can be hoped for is that the damage will have been halted for the future. (For this reason, paper clips or any other metallic fixing devices should never be used on a permanent basis!)

Perfectionists will tell you that, after they have been bleached, pictures should be rinsed in water to which size has been added, to restore what the bleaching process has removed. In practice, however, this applies only to the valuable prints on ancient types of paper which we have already recommended should be cared for by experts.

Mounting

Many decisions as to how pictures should be treated will be made in the light of how they are ultimately to be used. This is particularly true when it is a matter of deciding whether or not the pictures should be mounted.

Though we have spoken of the astonishing strength and durability of paper, the fact remains that pictures are very fragile things. To fix a thin and flimsy piece of paper on to a stouter, stronger card is an obvious way of protecting it, but the arguments for mounting are matched by arguments against.

Advantages of mounting

a) The picture is, henceforward, on a rigid card. This means that it can be more easily stored, particularly if the policy is to store it upright in a filing cabinet, facilitating inspection and reducing wear and tear caused by handling.

b) The mounting card will usually be larger than the picture mounted on it, thus providing a margin which will take the brunt of any wear and tear—scuffing as it is handled and filed, fingermarks and so forth.

c) The mounts can all be of a standard shape and size, so that pictures of varying sizes can be presented in a uniform manner. This makes storage and retrieval easier, and again reduces the chances of folding, creasing and other damage.

d) The extra width of the mount provides useful space for captioning, reference numbers and other data. This avoids the necessity for marking the picture itself.

e) The mounting card can itself be distinctive: it can be colour coded for purposes of filing, it can be easily identified as emanating from that particular library, or from a particular section of the library.

f) Effective mounting — particularly dry-mounting — improves the appearance of the picture by smoothing out folds and wrinkles. If the picture has had to be repaired, for instance by the imposition of patches or adhesive materials, these will be less conspicuous, and less liable to snag or catch on other items, if the picture is mounted.

Disadvantages of mounting

a) The best kinds of mounting are one-way methods: the picture will, quite simply, never be the same again. In the case of a really valuable item, where it is evident that it should be preserved in a state as close to its original condition as possible, any kind of mounting, and particularly dry-mounting, is likely to be out of the question.

b) Should damage occur after mounting, it is much more difficult to repair. The better the method used, the more difficult it is to remove the picture from its mount—as anyone knows who has tried to peel a dry-mounted picture from its backing.

In practice most picture librarians, if they decide to mount their material at all, will probably choose not to mount all of it. A library which provides its users with direct access to the material, involving a good deal of handling, will probably choose to mount all the material so available and this will be even more likely if the library permits users to take away the material on loan. On the other hand, libraries which hold material for reference only, and perhaps cater for a limited usership, may prefer to keep the pictures in their original state. For those libraries which do decide to mount their pictures, a choice of methods is available.

Hinges or other fixing devices can be placed at the upper two or at all four corners. This is effective in so far as it places the picture in juxtaposition with a stronger and larger item which will take the brunt of any wear and tear during handling. But that is all it does. This method is therefore suitable only for enhancing the protection of delicate items kept in horizontal storage, and which will not have to suffer very much handling.

Adhesive may be applied either at the corners or all over

45

the rear surface of the picture, which is then laid down on the card. This has the advantage of cheapness, but no other. Many adhesives, notably those which are petrol-based, will stain the picture in the course of time, and render the paper brittle and liable to crumble. Others, particularly water-based types and others whose adhesive effect is brought about by the evaporation of a liquid carrier leaving a chemical bonding substance behind, are liable to buckle the paper if it is anything but very stout, and this is often permanent. If the picture is of no great value—for instance, if it is just cut out from a modern periodical to give art students a convenient reference for an everyday item—then this will not matter and there is no point in choosing a more elaborate method.

If the picture is to be permanently mounted, dry-mounting is the only method which can be seriously recommended. This consists of pressing the picture on to its mount, with a sheet of adhesive tissue between them; the pressing is done by a heated press, and the process takes about ten seconds. Since the adhesive tissue must be trimmed to the size of the picture, and the two fixed to each other before being mounted on the card, it is a relatively elaborate process compared with those described above. It is also considerably more expensive, as the press must be purchased—the cost is between £100 and £200 according to size and sophistication—and the tissue naturally costs more than glue you squeeze out of a tube. However, the technique can become surprisingly fast once the operator gets the hang of it, and the results, in esthetic appearance and in practical utility, amply justify the outlay in time and money.

Care should also be taken to choose the right kind of card for mounting. It should be sufficiently rigid to stand upright in a filing cabinet, if that is the form of storage you decide on. But it must not be so rigid that it will not bend, for in that case it will be liable to crack—and when the mount cracks, the picture will crack with it. The question of shape and size will be discussed when we are considering retrieval methods.

Picture storage—general considerations
Almost all the functions of picture library are interdependent.

We have already seen that the answer to such questions as whether or not pictures should be mounted will vary according to the retrieval method chosen, a topic yet to be discussed; and the same applies even more forcefully to the method of storage adopted. At this stage, therefore, we shall concern ourselves only with general aspects of the question of storage.

Today there are scientific guidelines as to the optimum conditions for picture storage, but it is a fact that millions of pictures have survived for centuries without the benefit of such sophisticated advice. The fact is that pictures will put up with a great deal of abuse. Even if you were to soak a picture in water, then crumple it into a ball, it could probably be rescued and restored to very near its original state.

Nevertheless, there *are* some conditions which are better for your pictures than others, and a little care—most of it common sense—will see to it that the contents of the library are given a good chance of survival.

Temperature: Maintain a moderate ambient temperature, and keep it as constant as possible. Normal living/working levels are perfectly acceptable; it is the fluctuations which should be avoided. This applies particularly to libraries which close down over the weekend, where there is naturally a temptation to close down the heating also. In temperate climates this may not matter too much, but where the temperature is liable to fall precipitately, it is only sensible to instal some modest background heating so that a reasonable level is maintained.

Humidity: This is much more critical than temperature. Pictures should not be allowed to get too dry or too damp, for the first will dry up the paper and make it brittle, while the second may lead to mould and permanent damage. Here again, a wide margin is acceptable, but care should be taken to avoid violent fluctuations. Where the library is centrally heated, it may be advisable to instal humidifiers to maintain a balanced level between 55-65 percent.

Light: As a basic rule, all pictures should be exposed to light as little as possible. In the case of printed pictures, the effect of light will be minimal; but it will, nevertheless, cause deterioration in the paper. Direct sunlight, in particular, should be avoided.

Ventilation: In an efficient library, every part of the collection will be working for its living, so there should be no sections which are not visited periodically and the items flipped through or turned over. Where this is not the case, however—for instance, where there are reserve collections which may not get looked at from one year's end to another —it is good practice to visit them periodically and give them a bit of an airing, generally shake them up a little. Certain types of picture have a tendency to stick to their neighbours, but this can be prevented by separating them and replacing them in a slightly different order or position. Dust should not be allowed to accumulate, as this can attract insects and even larger vermin. And, of course, such periodic inspection will reveal if any more serious damage is occurring —if damp is creeping into some dark corner, or mice nibbling the corners off priceless etchings.

Accident: It may seem obvious, but care should be taken not to store pictures where they can easily be damaged. It is a nice idea to cheer up the place with potted plants, but potted plants need watering, which often means spills—so potted plants should never be kept over picture files. Coffee machines, glue pots, ink—all these are potential enemies which should be kept at a safe distance from pictures. And if there is the slightest risk of flooding, even from an overflowing sink, then pictures in the neighbourhood should never be stored on the floor.

FOUR

ACCESS AND RETRIEVAL

A picture is placed in a picture library only that it may be taken out again. From which it follows that, other things being equal—such as the well-keeping and security of the picture—the more rapidly it can be located and retrieved, the better organised that library can be said to be.

Principles
This does not mean that there is a single ideal system which is most desirable for every type of library. Once again we are in a situation where function and usership will determine decision making. And indeed, the decision as to what procedural technique to adopt for the purposes of retrieval is the most crucial, and the most far-reaching in its effects, that the picture librarian will have to make.

Fortunately, it is a decision which can be made by following a series of logical steps, at each of which a relatively simple question must be answered. The first of them is this: can those who will use the library be trusted to locate and retrieve the pictures themselves, or is this something that will be better done for them by a member of the library staff?

Sometimes the answer to this question will be immediately apparent. If the pictures are intrinsically valuable, then only professional or experienced persons can be trusted to handle them. If they are intrinsically worthless, then there may be little harm in letting anyone handle them. Of course there will be cases where the answer must be that the users can be trusted with some of the material but not with all of it; or alternatively, that some of the users can be trusted with the material, but not all of them.

Sometimes the fundamental character of the library will

imply the answer. If it is a professional library, accessible only to members of a society or professional body, then it can be presumed that all may be permitted access to the collection. If it is a collection designed to provide reference material for art students, again, the very purpose with which the collection was formed demands that access be as open as is possible. On the other hand, a collection formed with the primary object of safeguarding and preserving valuable or fragile material for scholarly purposes will almost certainly restrict access to those who can show good cause.

Thus the answer given to this initial question will immediately determine into which of the two fundamental procedural categories the library will choose to class itself: *closed-access* or *open-access*. It remains to consider the advantages and drawbacks of the two approaches, and how each is best translated into physical terms.

Closed-access

This will be the preferred method in any picture library where:

a) the material is intrinsically valuable.

b) the material is by its nature fragile or liable to damage, such as ephemera or maps or posters.

c) the material is necessarily arranged in such a way as to be confusing to the user: for instance, if the collection is made up of several autonomous sections rather than comprehensively integrated.

d) existing physical conditions make it impracticable to allow open access; for instance, if space is inadequate for the users to move freely, or where the material is housed in file systems whose *modus operandi* would not be readily understood by the average user.

e) the type of user could not be trusted to handle the material with sufficient care; for instance, small children.

f) the nature of the material is such that a user might take a disproportionate time locating a specific item; for instance, a collection of architectural drawings or shop plans.

g) for any reason it is not desirable to let the user have sight of material other than the item he wishes or has been authorised to see; for instance, government records and other sensitive material.

50

Sometimes these factors will apply only to certain sections of the collection, in which case the librarian may well decide to permit open access to some sections but impose closed access on others. For example:

a) Collections which contain some material of intrinsic value, some of none. For instance, a collection might contain both original and copied material, and might choose to restrict access to the first category but make the second as freely accessible as possible.

b) Collections which contain material of which some can readily be mounted, while some cannot. For instance, many picture libraries contain ephemera collections, which are often not suited for mounting. Even when open access is the general rule, an exception might be made in respect of the unmounted items.

c) Users might be allowed access to transparencies, which are easily protected and filed, but not to black and white material which is more vulnerable.

The cases described above are those in which a distinction is drawn between one category of material and another; but, as already suggested, there may be cases when the librarian will choose to draw a distinction between one class of user and another. For instance, in a college library it may be felt that faculty and graduates may be permitted open-access to the material, but that students cannot be fully trusted to treat the pictures with proper consideration.

That word 'trust' is really the key to the matter. For once a library has decided to permit open-access, it will—no matter how many safeguards it builds into its system—have to trust the user to some extent. As a result, there are certain to be some unfortunate consequences, however careful and conscientious the user. There will be misfiling because he takes out a picture, then decides it is not suitable and puts it back in what he believes, mistakenly, to be the right place; there will be wear and tear due to unfamiliarity with handling pictures; and, sadly, now and again there will be theft or malicious damage, even among the seemingly most respectable classes of users. And while all these things can also happen with staff, they will not happen nearly so often; closed-access has, in these respects at least, very considerable advantages.

51

Retrieval systems for closed-access
Closed-access has one fundamental drawback: a third element is introduced into the dialogue between the user and the picture he wants. As in a United Nations meeting, an interpreter comes between the speaker and the hearer.

Somehow, then, the closed-access system must be devised in such a manner that the user, desiring a given picture, will receive that picture even though he has to convey his request via a third party. What does this imply when we set about drawing up our blueprint for the system?

First, it implies that staff are employed who will be sufficiently intelligent to understand what the user has in mind, and to translate that in terms of an actual picture; or, alternatively, that there is a catalogue sufficiently detailed for the user himself to identify the picture he needs and convey his request to the staff. Ideally, the catalogue reference will be a visual one, in the form of a small-scale reproduction of the given picture; unfortunately, the cost of creating a comprehensive visual catalogue is generally prohibitive for most picture libraries, so that a detailed verbal description is substituted. This must be cross-indexed in sufficient detail for identification to be certain even when the user has only part of the necessary information.

It is evident that in either case a heavy burden will be placed on the staff, who must be of sufficient intelligence either to comprehend the user's spoken request, or to compile an adequate catalogue for him to use. While theoretically it would be possible, in the case of a static collection whose material was never augmented, to have employed high-calibre staff to compile the original catalogue and, thereafter, employ mere fetchers and carriers to retrieve the material when requested, in practice some degree of interpretation will always be required even for the best-compiled catalogue.

Second, the pictures themselves must be identified in such a way that they can rapidly and unequivocally be matched with the catalogue entry or with the user's verbal request. In physical terms, this means that the necessary information must be supplied together with the picture itself, in an instantly accessible form—either a catalogue reference number or a clear and concise description.

Third, the pictures must be stored in such a way that they can be inspected for identification purposes, with a minimum of handling either of themselves or of other items, and presented to the user in a form which calls for a minimum of additional procedure.

The sort of complication that might cause delay and/or confusion would be if the picture were stored in a non-transparent envelope with other items, so that the envelope would have to be opened and all its contents removed to see whether the item was there or had perhaps been removed for some other user or purpose; or if it was felt desirable that some kind of indication should be left in place of the removed item to indicate that it had been removed. Again, it might be decided that it should be presented to the user in some kind of container—a plastic wallet perhaps—which would minimise the risk of damage or loss. One could easily think up further such complications.

Given that the foregoing requirements have been met, procedures can be organised on common-sense lines.

Procedure by verbal request
The steps here are as follows:

a) User asks to see selection of portraits of Shakespeare.

b) Staff member goes to appropriate file, or to index indicating appropriate file, makes a judicious selection and brings it to the user, perhaps in some kind of protective file or container.

c) User inspects selection, perhaps returns all in which he is not interested, which the staff member then returns to file.

d) User makes what use he wishes of picture, which may involve copying or borrowing (discussed later in this book).

e) Picture is returned to the staff member for re-filing.

Procedure by catalogue entry
Here, the sequence is:

a) User consults catalogue, locates possible portraits of Shakespeare, notes reference number.

b) User fills in request slip, quoting reference number, hands it to a staff member.

c) Staff member uses slip to locate and retrieve material which is brought to the user as described above.

The question which of these two methods is to be preferred will depend on the size and nature of the material, and the type of user. For instance, a fine art reference library catering for art historians will expect its users to request items with specific details such as artist's name and picture title, which will make identification straightforward. On the other hand, a more general collection, such as the Victoria and Albert Museum, might receive requests from all kinds of users for all kinds of purposes—not simply art historians but also fashion designers in search of inspiration, stage designers requiring period references, commercial artists looking for attractive motifs for packaging.

Storage for closed-access

When only a limited number of trustworthy people are to have direct access to the files, considerably less care need be taken for the pictures' protection. The important thing is that it should be easy to locate and retrieve them.

As always, a problem is caused by large and fragile items, such as posters and ephemera; but the majority of pictures are likely to range in size between 10cm square and 30cm square, and so may quite easily be housed in, for instance, packets in suspended files in metal cabinets. (Very small pictures may be mounted on larger pieces of paper to avoid damage when placed alongside larger items.) There are various methods available: the pictures may be placed loose in the files—though this makes them liable to collect dust; or they may be housed in envelopes, one or more of which are placed in each file.

This, of course, means that every time a picture is required, the envelope must be removed from the file and its contents removed and flipped through; so, to avoid excessive handling, the number of items in each envelope should be kept as low as is practicable—perhaps twenty pictures per envelope would be a reasonable figure. On the outside of the envelope it should be indicated what pictures are inside, to avoid opening the envelope and removing the contents more often than necessary. Transparent plastic envelopes would make this less necessary, and a numerical coding, if the pictures are suitably filed, will also be helpful. The arrangement of the files themselves can be by subject, number or whatever classification system has been chosen: we shall be discussing this aspect in the next chapter.

The advantage of suspended files is that the pictures are stored vertically; this means that they are not piled one on top of another. Unfortunately, many pictures cannot be housed in vertical files, but must perforce be kept in some form of horizontal storage. This, if the pictures are referred to at all frequently, makes them especially liable to damage, for flipping through a stack of pictures, particularly if they are of various sizes and thicknesses, means inevitable wear and tear on the corners and edges, and sooner or later tears, folds and creases.

Consequently, when pictures are stored horizontally, the drawers or shelves should be of minimum depth, with as few items as possible piled on top of one another. Again, it is advantageous to keep them in batches inside envelopes or folders, which can perhaps be removed and the contents flipped through on a table.

Here, too, plastic envelopes or folders have obvious merits. It should be remembered that plastic tends to cause condensation. It is best to choose a stiff, flexible type—which will in any case give the best protection—and open-sided wallets are preferable to envelopes because they allow air to circulate more freely, even though this also means that they admit dust at the same time. Plastic is usually inert chemically and will not itself damage the picture. However, certain types of plastic are incompatible with certain types of adhesive, so care should be taken if the picture has been mounted, especially if the adhesive was a petrol-based one.

Certain classes of material can be most effectively stored in albums. The availability of albums of various sizes with see-through plastic pockets means that valuable or fragile items can be housed very conveniently, the whole album being produced for the user who asks to see the item. This has the merit that the picture itself need never be handled except when it has to be removed for any reason. Albums of this type have not been available for a sufficiently long period for us to know if there are any deleterious effects in the very long term, but it would appear that there are none, and that the item is preserved in a chemically inert state without risk of deterioration. Unfortunately, the albums themselves are costly; and any extensive use of them requires a substantial investment which can be justified only in relation to the value of the pictures they contain.

Open-access

Open-access—that is, a system whereby those who use the library have immediate and direct access to the files containing the pictures—has several advantages:

a) The user may see all relevant material, not merely that which is selected for him. This is particularly valuable when he has only a general notion of what he is looking for—for example, if he needs a suitable illustration for a book jacket, where design considerations will be just as critical as that of subject-matter—the library staff can hardly be expected to divine what he has in mind, nor can a verbal description or catalogue entry indicate whether a picture will be suitable for his purpose.

b) Open-access eliminates the need for a detailed catalogue, for the pictures are to a large degree their own catalogue provided they are intelligently filed and classified (see next chapter). This alone means an enormous saving in staff time, not only in preparing the original catalogue and keeping it up to date, but also in explaining to users how the catalogue works. This has the further, secondary advantage, that newly acquired material can go straight into the files without needing to pass through the cataloguing process, which in closed access libraries usually involves a permanent backlog of uncatalogued pictures waiting their turn.

c) Open-access dispenses with the need for a specific numerical identification system, for the pictures can be filed by subject alone. This again saves staff time and permits greater flexibility in classification.

d) Users can to a large degree do their own research with only minimal guidance from staff. Retrieval of pictures by staff is limited only to those items which for some reason cannot be stored in the open files—large, rare or fragile material. This means that the staff are relieved of much purely mechanical work; when they are called on for help, it will be for their superior knowledge and expertise. This means greater job satisfaction for the staff with obvious benefits in respect of morale.

e) Last, but assuredly not least, open-access facilitates serendipity; for, unless the user is resolutely single-minded in his search for a specific item, he will become aware of other material, whether related or not to his search, and happy accidents will inevitably occur which will result in the more rewarding use of the library.

Against these obvious advantages, there are certain drawbacks which must be accepted:

a) Wear and tear of pictures will inevitably be increased. This means that much greater care will have to be taken to safeguard the material, involving time and expense.

b) Equally inevitable, alas, will be theft, loss and even malicious damage. Again, precautions will need to be taken to keep this to a minimum.

c) Mis-filing will occur when users, with the best will in the world, remove an item, then replace it in the wrong place.

d) The entire system must be designed for users who may be unfamiliar with the library, necessitating much greater thought when planning the classificatory set-up.

e) Staff must be available to assist users when they first arrive, to explain the system to them, and be on hand throughout their visit, in case any difficulty should crop up.

It will be up to the individual librarian, in the light—as always—of the nature of his material and the character of his users, to evaluate these two sets of factors and decide which on balance is the most suitable system for his library.

Storage for open-access
If the library can live with the drawbacks listed above, then the open-access system dispenses with a great many of the picture librarian's problems and at the same time makes it more attractive to the user. The pictures can be presented like goods in a super market, and provided that the system has been properly thought out at the start, and kept up

consistently, life is much simpler for one and all.

Clearly, the method of storage is of fundamental importance. First of all, certain categories of material will have to be excluded from the overall system: these include the large, the rare and the fragile, all of which for obvious reasons require special treatment. (Later we shall consider what this implies, and how the worst effects of such segregation can be minimised.)

While the storage methods considered for the closed-access library in the 'Storage for closed-access' section (p.54) would be acceptable for a relatively small, highly specialised, open-access library, with restricted and trustworthy usership, they would not be practicable for a larger library open to a wider public. In the first place, they would involve too much physical handling of the material; in the second, they require an inordinately large amount of guidance from the staff. What is required is a system in which labels guide the user to files in which pictures are immediately visible, and where he can see each item at once without having to remove or open an envelope, box or wallet. In other words, the pictures must be filed loose, as individual items.

Well, of course, loose pictures are vulnerable to damage, particularly if they are of varying shapes and sizes. So it follows that all pictures intended for open access should be mounted as described in 'Mounting' (p. 44), on rigid but flexible cards of standard size. In practice, most pictures are sized less than 25 x 20 cm, which is the most favoured photographic size. Consequently a standard mount size slightly larger than this—approximately A4, in fact—will be ideal.

Such cards can be filed vertically, on their longer sides, in the drawers of A4 filing cabinets; they can be then flipped through by user or staff, rapidly and with a minimum of handling. Much of the time they can be seen sufficiently well without even having to be removed from the drawer. Larger guide cards will indicate which section of the drawer contains which pictures, so that the user will need to flip through only a small number; or, alternatively, he may remove the contents of a section to look through them more comfortably at a desk or table. The pictures should, of course, be captioned on the top edge of the mount facing the user, so that

58

a quick indication is given as to what the card holds. (Captioning will be discussed in greater detail later.)

There is no reason why the same method should not be used either for larger or for smaller items. If a library has a substantial collection of large items, such as nineteenth century music covers, then these can be satisfactorily mounted on cards of A3 or whatever size is appropriate, and filed in the same way.

As for transparencies, so long as these are stored either in individual wallets or multi-pack suspended wallets, there is no difficulty whatever in making these available for open-access.

Safeguards for open-access systems
There is no avoiding the fact that to place pictures on open-access is to place them at risk. To many librarians it will seem like an open invitation to theft and damage. However, so long as the librarian acts advisedly, and faces up to the risks from the start, the dangers can be kept to a minimum. These guidelines will help:

a) All parts of the library should be under constant, or at least frequent, supervision by the staff. A radial layout, in which each file can be seen from a central desk where there is always somebody working, is ideal; but, because it is wasteful of space, it is not often practicable. Nevertheless, the filing cabinets should be so arranged that the greatest possible number can be seen by the greatest number of staff members.

b) There should be staff available for information and assistance at all times. Much of the confusion resulting from open-access stems from the fact that users, timorous about disturbing staff unnecessarily, try to do everything themselves, resulting in misfiled pictures and misplaced files, and more handling of the material than is really necessary. The staff, when welcoming the user and explaining the system, should make it clear that they may be consulted at any time.

c) The exit from the library should be clearly visible, preferably with a member of the staff permanently located close by, so that no user can leave the library taking material with him, deliberately or inadvertently. Naturally, handbags and briefcases must not be taken to the files.

d) Smoking should of course be forbidden absolutely.

e) Food and drink, if provided—there *are* libraries which offer their visitors coffee—should be consumed away from the files.

f) The system should be fully explained to the user before he is allowed access to the files. If the library is very large or complex, an instruction sheet may be provided showing where files and other facilities are located. The user should be instructed not to replace a picture if he has any doubt about its right place.

In addition, there are certain safeguards which apply to any kind of library where the material is of value and where there is any chance that the material, the service or the facilities may be abused in any way. In such cases it is customary to require that the user produce evidence of identity, and explain the reason for his visit, and perhaps produce some kind of authority such as a note from his employer, publisher, director of studies etc. The major public collections require would-be users to start by making application for a reader's ticket, which must be produced when using the library.

FIVE

CLASSIFICATION AND CATALOGUING

THE differences between administering a book library and a picture library emerge most critically when it comes to classifying the material.

Both book and picture libraries may be used either for specific or for non-specific requests. Just as a user may ask for Burton's *Anatomy of Melancholy* without needing to inspect it first or being willing to accept a substitute, so he may request Durer's *Melancolia*. Contrariwise, just as he may browse through the medical section of a book library until he finds a history of nineteenth century medicine which looks as though it will tell him what he wants to know, so he may flip through representations of Victorian hospitals till he finds one which says what he wants it to say.

Principles

At first sight, then, it might be thought that a classification scheme suitable for a book library would be equally suitable for a picture library. Both pictures and books alike may span the full gamut of human knowledge, experience and imagination.

It only takes a second thought, however, to see that in practice the reverse is closer to the truth. In a sense, words and pictures divide the world between them. There are areas where words do a better job of communication, and others where the contrary applies. Metaphysical speculation, for example, is a subject that almost totally resists any attempt at visual expression, whereas verbal accounts of architectural styles or the vicissitudes of female fashion will be woefully inadequate compared with pictorial representations.

Nevertheless, it may be argued that the kind of all-inclusive formal classification scheme generally used in book libraries is intended to be universal in its application, and surely will comprehend any subject likely to be found in a picture library? This is, indeed, the case; and if the only criterion were to devise a system of compartments into which the pictures could be neatly tucked away, such systems would be perfectly appropriate. But a library is not a repository, it is a living instrument designed to be used; and the way it is used varies from one picture library to another. This is why picture librarians have found, in practice, that off-the-shelf classification systems do not generally meet their needs, and that an *ad hoc* system, related to the specific collection and the specific usership of the individual library, is the effective solution in most cases.

The point can be well illustrated by taking a simple example, a collection of fine art pictures. Strictly speaking, there is no reason why a collection of reproductions of fine art should not be organised in just the same way as a book library on the same subject: the material is subdivided first according to the medium in which the artist is working; then according to the period; then according to the country or culture in which he was working; then by individual artists or groups of artists. These classes may of course be arranged in a different hierarchical order: some librarians might feel that the regional classification should be primary, others that a straight alphabetical order, subsequently subdivided, best meets their users' needs; but the fundamental principle remains the same. To back up this basic classification there will of course need to be an alphabetical index, in case the user has forgotten whether Mantegna is a modern Spanish or a renaissance Italian artist; and a title index, in case he cannot for the moment recall whether it was Rossetti or Millais who painted *The Boyhood of Raleigh*.

So far, so good, and for the purposes of most art students and historians, such classification is probably adequate. But then along comes a designer who is collecting material for an exhibition at the Victoria & Albert Museum on the subject of gardens. He is sadly short of pictures of gardens in the fifteenth century, and would like to find portraits which show gardens in the background, through doors, or even reflected in mirrors. . . Clearly, to meet the needs of such users, an elaborate subject index is called for.

Most picture librarians would recognise the desirability of a subject index, even though they may not be able to see their way to implementing it without taking on several extra staff and devoting countless man-hours to the project. And even if their budgets could be made to stretch to accommodate such an effort, they would have to face the fact that they could not possibly cross-index *every* ingredient in *every* picture. In other words, they would have to be selective and, naturally, the selection would be based on the type of request generally received from the specific usership of that library.

If this is true of what is perhaps the simplest of all types of picture libraries, how much more is it true of one where the subject matter is infinitely diverse, where the medium in which the artist worked and even his identity are secondary in importance, or even totally irrelevant, to the subject itself.

Consequently, I have not the slightest hesitation in saying that, for the great majority of picture libraries, the only valid approach to classification is to start by considering the nature of the collection and the character of the usership (which, as we have seen continually throughout the preceding chapters, are wholly interdependent, the one dictating or being dictated by the other). This will, I suggest, provide the only sure touchstone as to which sections of the library should be kept general and which minutely subdivided; in which order hierarchical classification structures should be presented; what type of signposting and cross-reference is required; how formal or how informal nomenclature should be; and all the many variables which require decision-making on the part of the library staff.

Ad hoc *systems*
It may be said, and with logical justification, that to refer to an *ad hoc* system is to perpetrate a contradiction in terms. The very fact that a classification method adopted by a picture library is specific to its own needs and no other, and is infinitely flexible and liable to modification if the nature

of the usership should require it, is inherently opposed to what is normally meant by the word 'system'—perhaps a more appropriate word would be 'arrangement'. However, this is a semantic point; rightly or wrongly I shall continue to use the word 'system' to refer to the way pictures are arranged in a library, even though it is continually changed from one day to the next and is based on no formal structure whatever.

Nevertheless, that objection highlights the fundamental drawback of such a pragmatic approach: nobody who visits the library will be familiar with the system, and it will have to be explained to each visitor. However, in practice this is true of all classification systems; even a library which has followed faithfully the guidelines of the Smith System or the Jones System cannot assume that all those who use the library will be familiar with that system, and the only ones who will benefit will be the staff.

The test of the efficacy of the system, then, will be the amount of explanation needed to be given to the visitor, and the ease with which the newcomer adapts to it. This in turn will be affected by how large the library is, how well administered it is, how good the staff are at explaining the system, and how well signposted the contents are.

Throughout the greater part of this book it has been possible to indicate general practice without reference to particular libraries and individual usages have been cited only by way of illustrating general principles. But in this chapter, for the reasons set out above, it is necessary to depart from this practice, since the very essence of the type of system we are discussing requires that it shall be geared to the needs of an individual library, and if the discussion is to be at all useful it must be illustrated by something more than vague principles.

Consequently, the approach taken by an individual library has been taken as a paradigm, on the understanding that no other library is likely to have precisely the same type of material or usership, and would have to modify such a system to a greater or lesser degree to use it for their own purposes. But then it is not suggested that this should be done; rather, I want to encourage, by force of example, other picture

64

librarians to build up their own system. The one described here is appropriate to a particular type of collection and a particular type of user; it cannot be taken as a model except by another picture library which happens to find itself in precisely the same situation, which is highly unlikely. At the same time, it may well suggest how a different library could set about approaching its own parallel problem.

It should, perhaps, be added that this particular library has worked with this system for some fifteen years; that users of the library, even on their first visit, can usually master the system in its broad essentials in a minute or two, needing guidance from the staff only for the more esoteric ramifications of the collection; that the staff, who have to use it (and who modify it continually as circumstances require), find it effective from their point of view; and finally, that professional librarians and students of librarianship, visiting the library in the course of surveys, studies and so forth, have unanimously agreed that this form of pragmatic approach is valid, at least for a picture library of this type. In other words, whatever the system about to be described may or may not do, it certainly *works*.

The library in question is an all-picture library, though the individual pictures are supplemented by a substantial quantity of material in books, periodicals and albums. The 'core' of the collection is made up of individual pictures, mounted on card and filed vertically in A4 filing cabinets, as described earlier in this book.

The collection is a historical one, containing virtually no material more recent than 1939. Apart from this limitation, it is completely general in scope, covering every subject and every type of material. In addition, it contains some special collections, comprising copies of material in other archives which are made available through this library for greater convenience and, though their particular provenance is indicated on the picture mount, this material is completely integrated with the rest of the collection.

While it is recognised that certain types of special collections might have to be kept on their own, particularly if they are very substantial in size, as a general rule this should be avoided, and the material integrated with the rest of the collection. To do otherwise adds substantially to the burden on the staff and leads to confusion for the user.

The material held in the library comprises:

a) original prints and engravings of all shapes and sizes

b) photographic copies of the above (normally 25 x 20 cm)

c) original photographs of all shapes and sizes

d) photographic copies of the above

e) colour transparencies made from originals of various kinds; standard size 9 x 6 cm

f) postcards

g) cigarette cards

h) greetings cards

i) ephemera of all kinds, including—for example—trade cards, advertising items, cheques, funeral announcements, catalogues, licences, theatre programmes, wartime ration books, tickets, menus etc

j) pictures contained in books, periodicals, store catalogues, advertising brochures etc

k) photographic copies of the above

Given such a diversity of material, how is order established? First, the decision has to be made which of the items can be accommodated physically under an overall umbrella, the main library, and which categories should be excluded and given special treatment. It should go without saying that the latter course should be adopted only where absolutely necessary, and as far as possible the material should be integrated into a single comprehensive whole. In this instance, the following decisions were made:

Original prints: Those of no great intrinsic value are mounted and filed as already described. Those which are of . substantial value, or are too fragile or too large for such a course are housed elsewhere, in large-drawer cabinets or albums where they are available for inspection on request, but are not normally on open-access. Those items which are regarded as certain, sooner or later, to be requested by the users of the library—for instance, Kip's 1712 view of Longleat—are photographed at once; others can be photographed on request. (See chapter on copying later.) All items of any significance are cross-referenced within the open files (see chapter on cross-referencing later).

Ephemera: The same practice is true of ephemera, which does not lend itself to storage in the standard files and is often very fragile. Again, many items have been photographed and these copies are of course filed in the usual way. Wherever possible, ephemera items are stored in albums for easy inspection; the rest are kept in drawers. Here too, the material is cross-referenced from the open files.

Special collections: As already indicated, these are integrated with the main collections; the material is, however, mounted on a different colour card and carries a label clearly indicating its special character. One example is a collection of family photographs relating to a certain eminent psychologist. This obviously results in an inordinate amount of material in the portrait file when his name is reached, which might surprise the user, except that such anomalies are encountered throughout a picture library as those who use them soon discover. Thus, in any section devoted to book illustration, there has to be an entire drawer for the letter D simply because Charles Dickens was so well served by his illustrators; while his neighbour, Dostoievski, sulks in un-illustrated oblivion.

Colour transparencies, which cannot conveniently be housed along with the 25 x 20 cm cards, are kept in their own independent section, but every effort is made to keep the classification system parallel with the main system, so that the user will find material organised in just the same way when he passes from one to the other. There are, of course, certain areas where the proportions will vary: most fashion plates, for example, are in colour, whereas industrial scenes from historical periods were virtually always in black and white.

Books and periodicals: These cannot, of course, be integrated in any way with the main collection. Here again a system of cross-referencing is adopted, so that while looking through the main files, the user's attention is brought to the fact that there is supplementary material in this or that book or magazine. Such referencing procedures are described in greater detail later.

It will be seen that the user can obtain access to the greater part of the library's material by going to the two parallel systems, the mounted cards for black and white material and the transparencies which in this library are housed in individual plastic wallets. Such exceptions as exist are indicated by reference cards housed along with the main collection.

So except in matters of detail, all a user needs to know before starting to use the library—apart from procedural matters regarding conditions of use and loaning arrangements —is how to find his way round the primary collections. The primary breakdown is into:

PEOPLE
PLACES
EVENTS
TRANSPORT & TRAVEL
SCIENCE, TRADE AND INDUSTRY
SPORT & ENTERTAINMENT
NATURE
BEHAVIOUR
DAILY LIFE

These in turn comprise the following sub-divisions:

PEOPLE

Portraits, alphabetically arranged. It is found helpful to give people for whom a considerable quantity of material exists a sub-section to themselves with its own marker card; others are simply filed alphabetically. In some cases there are special exceptions: for example, all Byron's mistresses are filed together with Byron, the argument being that this relationship was their chief claim to the notice of posterity, and that a majority of researchers who are interested in one will also be interested in the others; it is, therefore, a useful time-saver to group them together, but it is recognised that this is a special usage which is related to the type of user who visits this particular library. The same result could be achieved to a lesser extent by having a cross-reference card under BYRON directing the user to the various ladies in their strict alphabetical homes; but in this instance the reverse policy has been adopted, and it is in the proper files that the cross-reference cards are to be found.

Problems arise, of course, in the case of titled persons.

The normal practice in most biographical dictionaries is to list such people by their family name; but in this library it is appreciated that most people are likely not to know the family name of, say, the Earls of Durham or Derby, and are more likely to be looking for them under their title. However, this course is not followed systematically: both Robert Walpole and Benjamin Disraeli are best known under their family names rather than their titles, and are so filed. Again, this flexible approach is part of the pragmatic policy followed by this individual library in view of the nature of its usership, and it is not suggested that the same principle should be followed by, say, a picture library attached to a college of heraldry.

Royalty is housed separately, by country. Difficulties arise as to when the royal blood is running so thin that the individual should really be consigned to join the common herd: this can only be done on a somewhat arbitrary basis. Thus in this library, Austrian Archdukes and Spanish Infantas and French Dauphins and English Princes count as royalty, and so do all those Margraves and Electors and Landgraves of old Germany; but Dukes, however royal, and American Presidents and Dutch Stadtholders, are denied royal status. Popes are regarded as royalty *ex gratia*, no distinction being made between spiritual and material kingdoms.

Costume is filed chronologically in this section, as being more closely related to the theme of 'people' than any other. Racial types likewise, though here the subdivisions are regional.

PLACES

Most of this section can be organised on a simple hierarchical basis: first by continent, then by individual country, then by individual town or other feature. Along with each country, where appropriate, are separate subdivisions for special aspects:

Archeology in that country.

Homes of famous people and royalty (alphabetically by name).

General scenes with no specific indication: for instance, a print showing a typical Kaffir village or a town in the American West.

Maps and plans.

EVENTS

It is self-evident that historical events should be filed in chronological order. It is less evident how they should be sub-divided, and whether the sub-dividing should occur before or after the chronological process. For instance, it might be considered a valid approach to arrange the entire collection in chronological order, year by year or century by century, and then subdivide by geographical area, or some other subject classification such as cultural events, political events and the like, as appropriate.

In the case of our model library, the decision was taken to start by dividing the material geographically, putting into regional files all items which related to that region alone, or to that region predominantly, and establishing parallel files for items which related to more than one region—such as an international agreement or war. The following notes show how some of the problems were resolved:

a) Countries which contained a sufficient number of pictures were filed separately: this applied to, for instance, Britain, France, China, Russia etc.

b) Countries too small to contain a substantial number of pictures were grouped; for example, West Indies, Balkans, Pacific Islands.

c) Civil wars were filed with the country concerned, but international wars were filed separately; for instance, the Crusades, the Hundred Years' War, the Franco-Prussian War. Colonial wars were regarded as pertaining only to the country in which they were fought—for instance, the Ashanti, Zulu and Boer wars were regarded as being purely African in relevance. However, the Franco-Prussian War, which was fought entirely on French soil, was regarded as international in character, so that the actual location of the battlefronts should not be regarded as a criterion!

d) Ancient cultures were usually given separate treatment: for instance, Prehistory (before and subsequent to the emergence of man), Ancient Rome, Ancient Greece, and the events narrated in the Bible which, for the purposes of classification, were regarded as history. Some of these decisions were necessarily arbitrary. Had the collection contained a substantial quantity of material relating to the ancient Sumerian or Cretan civilisations, for instance, separate files would have been established for them; as it happens, the quantity of material did not warrant this and, consequently, what material we had was filed with Asia and Greece respectively.

e) Exploration was housed along with the country or region concerned, but frequently given separate sub-divisions when the amount of material warranted it.

Within each regional division, the material was arranged in a straight historical manner; though in view of the broad scope of this particular collection, no attempt was made to break down the material into time-spans of less than one year. Had the collection contained substantial material on recent political events, it might have been necessary to further sub-divide the material chronologically; and, indeed, the wealth of material on, say, France or Germany in 1848, or Italy in 1860, almost warrants this as it is. However, the task of going through a few dozen pictures is not so great as to justify the labour of establishing dates by month, which are not always supplied by the publishers of the original material.

Having arranged the material by region and date, the question of subdivision arose. Whereas the basic chronological arrangement was suitable to the mass of material—for instance, the history of the United States between 1865 and the outbreak of war in 1917 could be subdivided by markers at ten-year intervals, with no further subdivision—it was found that variations on this approach were more convenient in special cases. Here are some examples:

Events in British history were arranged not by neat centuries but by the dates of the reigning monarch. This was a purely pragmatic decision which could not be justified by any *a priori* argument but is certainly appropriate to the type of visual material normally available for the documentation of British history up to the nineteenth century, where historians—and consequently, the publishers of historical illustrations—have always treated history in terms of kings and queens.

Particular episodes or events were given their own individual sub-divisions, extracted from the main chronological sequence but placed in juxtaposition. This again was a purely

71

pragmatic decision, based on the type of request received and the type of material available. Such sub-divisions included:

a) Civil wars such as those in England in the 1640s and the United States in the 1860s.

b) Political events such as the Dreyfus Affair in France, the Mary Queen of Scots Affair in Britain.

c) The careers of eminent persons whose life histories were inseparable from that of their country, such as Luther in Germany.

d) Aspects of a country's history which tend to be treated as areas of special interest, such as French, German and Italian involvement on the African continent, or the opening up of the western territories of the United States.

e) Particular events which, quite simply, have attracted a particularly large quantity of visual documentation, for instance the Norman invasion of Britain in 1066, the Spanish Armada of 1588, Napoleon III's *coup d'etat* in France in 1851, the voyages of Cristoforo Columbus, and so on.

By now it will be evident that, whatever classification scheme is adopted, the actual implementation of that scheme will involve a great many pragmatic decisions in the interests of convenience. Furthermore, these decisions will continually be added to as new material comes into the library: the sudden arrival of a batch of material relating to the career of Garibaldi, for example, might well cause the library staff to create a special file. Consequently, whatever system is adopted at the outset, it must not be so rigid that it will be awkward to carry out such modifications. In our model library, such changes take place in one section of the library or another almost daily, as new facets of a subject are singled out for individual treatment.

TRANSPORT AND TRAVEL
Most of the material in this section can be conveniently filed under main headings:
SEA & WATER TRANSPORT
Boats and ships of various types.
Aspects of water transport such as naval reviews, ship construction, regattas, raising wrecks, passengers and their accommodation.

Docks, canals, lighthouses etc.
ROAD
Man-powered, animal-powered and mechanical: then sub-
divided as appropriate into trams, buses, private and public
carriages etc.
RAIL
Basic aspects, for instance locomotives, rolling-stock, con-
struction, accidents.
Railway history in various regions.
Special railway types, for instance underground, funiculars,
monorails.
FLIGHT AND SPACEFLIGHT
Non-dirigible, airships, powered aircraft.
Special types, for instance, birdmen.
Space exploration in fiction, fantasy and fact.
Unidentified flying objects.
ENGINEERING ASSOCIATED WITH TRANSPORT
Bridges, tunnels etc.
TRAVEL
Basic aspects, subdivided by region, for instance:
Travel in Egypt.
Seaside.
Hotels.
Emigration, subdivided by region.
It has also been found helpful to include special sections
for 'British Abroad' and 'Other Europeans Abroad', simply to
meet demand for such material: a perfect example of prag-
matism at work.

SCIENCE, TRADE AND INDUSTRY
Moving into more diverse spheres of activity, it becomes less
easy to formalise the arrangement. Our model library includes
in this category the following sections:
INDUSTRY
Mining and manufacture of various commodities, of which
the more important—metals, textiles, coal—have main sections
of their own; the second rank—ceramics, blacksmiths, rope-
making—have sub-sections; the remainder—gutta-percha, alum,
artificial flowers—are simply arranged alphabetically. The
division into main sections or otherwise is based purely on

73

the quantity of material.
Working conditions, including child labour.
Factory buildings, exterior and interior, by region.
Machines and tools.
Power supply.
Instruments: it is recognised that there is a strong overlap here with Science, and no alternative has been found but to locate the file reasonably close to both Industry and Science and hope that researchers concerned with instruments in relation to one and the other will both find their way to it.

TRADE AND COMMERCE
Shops and markets.
Auctions, pawnbrokers, sales.
Street trades.
Banks and financial subjects.
Trade, by region.
Stock and commodity exchanges.
Money *per se*—bank notes, coins and other currency; misers.

COMMUNICATIONS
Reading, writing, libraries.
Printing.
Press—reporting, publishing, selling, reading.
Primitive communications systems, such as smoke signals and beacons.
Postal services, by region.
Telephone.
Telegraph, ocean cables etc.

SCIENCE
Research and applications.
Contributions made by individual scientists, by name.
Astronomy—observatories, equipment.

NATURAL PHENOMENA
Alphabetical sequence from Aurora to Volcano, with general sections for Geology and Meteorology, also—pragmatism again—Seasons and Scenery (the latter subdivided into Land, Sea, River, Lake etc).

FARMING
Main sections—dairy farming, agriculture, horticulture.
Regional sections.
Equipment.

Also included in this section, though somewhat diffidently, are the following sections which should clearly go together, and have a clear relationship to Industry, but ties no less strong elsewhere:
BUILDING
Architectural styles, formal.
Building styles, chronologically arranged.
Building styles, regional.
Interiors.
Furniture.
Lighting.
Heating.

ART, ENTERTAINMENT, SPORT
This section loosely gathers various cultural and leisure pursuits:
ART
General aspects, such as techniques.
Examples of art, filed by artist.
Galleries.
EXHIBITIONS
MUSEUMS
APPLIED ART
Ornament, including ornamental alphabets, borders etc.
Heraldry.
Art objects, such as ornamental silverware etc.
ENTERTAINMENT
Sections for various types, such as circus, music hall, puppets, street performers, black and white minstrels, fairs etc.
Theatre, including scenes from plays by title, portraits of actors, theatre buildings, back-stage scenes, stage sets and furniture etc.
MUSIC
Historical sections, opera, instruments.
DANCING
GAMES
Including toys and tricks.
MECHANICAL ENTERTAINMENT DEVICES
Gramophones, cinema, television.

SPORT
Subdivided into the various forms.

NATURE
Practice here will vary crucially between the picture library
catering for the scientist or specialist, and one which is only
having to meet the needs of art students and designers. The
first will probably follow some formal classification scheme,
perhaps based on latin nomenclature, and recognising that
spiders and marmosets and narwhals are all members of
various families. A high degree of organisation is called for
in view of the fact that, to date, taxonomists have identified
some million and a half species of living organisms, and are
adding a further ten thousand to the list every year: there
are nearly ten thousand kinds of birds and, even though
scientists believe that we have not yet discovered half the
marine organisms sharing the planet with us, some 150,000
have been identified.

In the face of such figures, probably a majority of picture
libraries will shrink from the scientific approach and be happy
to file Beetles, Deer, Finches and so on by simple everyday
labels. Sub-sections will also be required for:
Hunting, including poaching, falconry etc.
Fishing, distinguishing between that which is done for food
and that done for sport; you will have to decide whether
whaling is hunting or fishing for yourself.
Plants, vegetables, fruit, herbs and spices.
Gardening, forestry.
Zoos and other animal homes.

DAILY LIFE AND BEHAVIOUR
If it was hard to prescribe valid guidelines in other parts of
the library, it is next to impossible to do so when we come to
the multitudinous activities which make up the daily lives of
the human race, whether on an everyday or an occasional
basis. Our model library, for better or worse, has opted for
the following categories:
CRIME
Includes all apsects of law, punishment, prisons, and has
special sections for pirates, highwaymen etc.

CUSTOMS
Some classified by season of the year, such as Christmas
and harvest festivals;
Others by region of the world, such as Africa, France;
Others by their place in the human life-cycle, such as birth
ceremonies, marriage customs, funeral rites.
The distinction between customs and religious practices is
utterly impossible to draw, for even experienced anthro-
pologists might argue as to which springs from the other.
Again, the only answer is to place the sections adjacent to
one another and hope for the best.
EDUCATION
FAMILY LIFE
With sub-divisions for aspects of human life which are not
part of family life but are defined by not being so, such as
'old maids', bachelor life, widowhood etc.
Includes children and child-rearing.
FOOD AND DRINK
HOUSEHOLD
Includes domestic activities such as laundry, removals,
cleaning the house, dressing, toilet etc.
MEDICAL
Includes physiological subjects such as anatomy.
MILITARY
Includes weapons, duels, tournaments and—for want of
anywhere better to put them—scenes showing civilians
fighting one another in anger as opposed to sport.
OCCULT
Includes various aspects of the paranormal.
POLITICS
RELIGION
Includes such themes as anti-semitism which are based on
religious practices.
SEX
Includes women's rights, prostitution, and just plain pictures
of pretty girls.
The foregoing is not intended as a comprehensive analysis
of the classification system that might be adopted by a
picture library. Even the individual library that has been
chosen as a model contains hundreds, perhaps thousands, of

categories and sub-categories which have not been mentioned. All that this summary has set out to do has been to indicate a possible way of breaking down the material into convenient divisions.

It could have been done many others ways. For example, the entire library could be arranged on an alphabetical basis— ADVERTISING, AIRCRAFT, ANIMALS, ARMS—which would mean that any user, as soon as he had established the appropriate word (Feminism or Suffragettes or Womens rights?), could find his way directly to the category he needed, without having to ponder as to whether it pertained to science rather than entertainment, as might be the case with, say, radio or photography.

Again, a library with a certain type of material or usership might find that it meets requests best by having the material filed by region, again subdivided into spheres of interest— history, social conditions, ethnic types and so forth. Such an arrangement might well be the most effective for an organisation like OXFAM or the United Nations.

Whatever system is adopted, there are always going to be overlaps—between religion and customs, between politics and places (where do parliament buildings go? And do you separate exteriors, which form part of a townscape, and interiors, which may show political activities taking place?) and between transport and sport (what about the Oxford and Cambridge boat race?). Also, there will be awkward subjects which do not properly fit in any one section rather than another—slavery is a notably awkward example, and *objects d'art*, archeology and duels are all thorns in any classifier's flesh.

Unhappy decisions will have to be made, too, with such questions as street scenes—when the scene is clearly related to street repair or maintenance, it ought surely to go into transport; whereas, if it shows crowds thronging London Bridge, it belongs more in some social category. Radio as used in the home is clearly entertainment—but not when it is being used to broadcast an SOS message for a ship in distress. A flood caused by act of God can comfortably be classed as a natural phenomenon—but who is to blame when a dam bursts, God or the contractor? And if unburst dams are securely housed along with water supply, what is the point of putting them somewhere else when they crack, even though the consequence is a flooded valley and thousands of deaths. . . . ?

Well, of course, one could go on for ever—such problems are the challenge which the librarian has to face, and, like many other forms of challenge, one of the most enjoyable aspects of the subject.

Clearly, though, and understandably, any well-trained librarian will be appalled at the apparently hit-and-miss approach which has been taken in the foregoing section. At the same time, any librarian who can add a few years' practical experience to his basic training will appreciate the advantages of some such pragmatic approach. Probably every single instance listed above could have been decided in a different way; no universal validity is claimed. All that can be hoped is that, after skimming through this section, the librarian will have the courage to forge his own classification system and let it be tempered in the real world of daily usage.

Captioning
Clearly every picture should have on it the basic information about it which will be required by the staff who have to put it in its proper place in the library, and by the user who needs to identify it. It will not need to carry complete information—this would be impossible, for who can know in advance what information about a picture is likely to be required—but should indicate where further information may be obtained. Consequently, the following data should be provided:

Data required for filing the picture: According to the system adopted, this may be either numerical or verbal, and according to the size and complexity of the library it can be summary or highly specific. For example, if all the pictures in the library are reproductions of works of art, then the basic information of artist and title will itself be sufficient for filing purposes; on the other hand, if some formal system is used, then some kind of numerical classification may be imposed to which all individual items are subservient, so that a staff filer need not look at the picture or take any note of its content, but simply register that it carries the number 7/3/42, which means that he has to take it to filing cabinet number 7, open the third drawer from the top, and insert the picture in sub-section number 42. From a sheer mechanical efficiency viewpoint, this may well be highly effective in terms of staff labour. However, it is no way to familiarise the staff with the contents of the collection, and is of value only where those who have to do the picture filing are menial dogsbodies employed for that purpose alone and, particularly, are not liable to be called upon by the users of the library for guidance. While, doubtless, libraries exist which are content to employ such mindless zombies, pending the perfection of the robot, such a practice is to be deplored.

There is another reason against using a numerical classification system, which is that it is easy to make a typing mistake with numbers. It is easy to make a typing mistake with words too, of course; but, whereas it is easy to see that if someone has typed HAMILYON, LADY, the chances are they mean HAMILTON, LADY, a number that has been mis-typed may well pass unnoticed. And it cannot be said too often that a picture mis-filed is a picture lost.

Consequently, a verbal description of some kind is desirable. Clearly, if this can be combined with some information about the picture which will be of use to the user, two purposes will have been served at once.

Basic information about picture content: This can include a series of data in hierarchical order, indicating the various categories and sub-categories which will guide the user to the individual picture just as they will guide the filer to the right place to file it. For example:
FOOD AND DRINK // COOKING APPLIANCES / BAIN-MARIE

EVENTS IN BRITAIN // CIVIL WAR / CHARLES RAISES STANDARD AT NOTTINGHAM 1642

These items of information should be located on the front of the card, and on the top (assuming, this is, that a mount is being used, and that space has been left round the picture adequate for such information). This will mean that the picture does not have to be removed from the file in order that its content may be identified; the user can simply flip through the filed cards until he sees the subject he is after, and he can then examine the picture itself to see whether it meets his needs. Ideally, the basic information referred to above will be written in a single line across the top of the card.

In the case of the model library described above, this captioning is done by hand. This seems laborious, and unlikely to be consistently neat; but it has the advantage that the caption can be written directly on to the card. However, if the information is typed, this will have to be on to an adhesive label, which is then affixed to the card (and can, of course, be peeled off again—a mixed blessing). Alternatively, a card may be chosen which is sufficiently flexible to be typed on, but in that case it is unlikely to be sufficiently rigid for filing purposes. (Come to think of it, why has nobody invented a typewriter which will type on to flat surfaces?) There is an added aspect to the question of captioning by hand: it gives a 'human' touch to the pictures which will be welcomed by some libraries, deplored by others —yet another case for the individual decision.

It will be seen that the caption is sub-divided into clauses. These separate the succeeding steps in the classification hierarchy, the main section being indicated by a separation in the form of a double oblique stroke, the subdivisions indicated by single strokes. It is evident that in the case of a very complex subject, the number of hierarchical steps could be carried to horrific lengths—for example, if this principle were strictly adhered to, one might come across a picture captioned:

TRANSPORT // SHIPS / REGIONAL / BRAZIL / BALSA RAFT / STEERING MECHANISM

or

RELIGION // PROTESTANTISM / BRITAIN / NONCON-FORMIST SECTS / QUAKERS / PERSECUTION / JAMES NAYLOR IN PILLORY

81

In such cases, common-sense may be allowed to prevail, on the principle that so long as the objects are attained—that the user can be expected to locate it and the staff to correctly file it—the system can be modified in any way that makes life easier for the captioner.

Certain practices can help to make the above method of captioning more effective. When captioning portraits of individuals, the name of the individual should be written on the right hand side of the card rather than the left. This may seem perverse, but the rationale is sound, as it means that a name such as:

ESSEX, ROBERT DEVEREUX, SECOND EARL OF

can be written

ROBERT DEVEREUX' SECOND EARL OF ESSEX

as it should properly be, and with the result that the key-word ESSEX appears at the top-right corner of the card where it will most easily catch the eye. Indeed, for even greater clarity, I recommend that the name should be written thus.

ROBERT DEVEREUX, Second Earl of ESSEX

but these are minor usages which each library must develop to meet its own preferences and necessities.

When captioning pictures for which the date is all-important, notably historical events, this should be included among the basic information at the top of the picture; again, it is probably best located at the top right of the mount, separated from the rest of the caption.

The important thing with such usages as these is that they should be adhered to without exception, so that all who work in or use the library come to take them for granted. Thus, when exceptions are made, it will be seen at once that they *are* exceptions, and not mistakes. Thus it may be felt that the date of a fashion plate is all-important, and the date is positioned prominently, at the beginning of the caption, thus:

The information considered so far has been that required for filing, retrieval and subject identification. But there are also descriptive data which ought always to accompany the picture:

The source of the picture: Our model library places this information at the lower left of the card, away from the main caption, and following the tradition of the old printmakers. The information will vary according to the type of item: here are some examples:

Sidney Paget in the 'Strand Magazine'
Basire, after Reynolds
Leipzig Illustrirte Zeitung
Anonymous woodcut
Harleian MS 153/82

The actual extent of the information supplied will depend on what, in practice, those who habitually use the library show a need to know. In the case of a fine art collection, for example, the provenance of the original work of art may be significant.

The date when the picture was made or published: Some confusion is apt to creep in here, for it will often happen that the date of creation of the picture is not the same as the date of the event depicted in the picture—for example, a nineteenth century artist's representation of the defeat of the Spanish Armada. In such a case, if the practice suggested above has been followed, the date 1588 will appear at the top right of the card; it will only disturb the uneducated user of the library if he also sees a second date 1885 at the bottom of the card. It is, therefore, recommended that if this information is supplied at all, it should be in brackets after the title of the publication, thus:

CASSELL'S HISTORY OF ENGLAND (1885)

But when it may be presumed that the date of publication is also the same, or close to the same, as the scene depicted, then the date should be presented more positively; and for this purpose it may be convenient to use the lower right hand corner of the card. When the date of the picture is not known, a guess should wherever possible be made, for even the roughest guide (eg circa 1840) is better than nothing. The librarian should remember that even though he may not be able to date a picture, he will probably be able to give an approximate date to within a decade or so, and this is likely to be much more than most of those who use his library will be able to do.

To summarise, then, if the form of captioning recommended here is adopted, a typical card will carry the following information and in the following way:

Top left	SPORT // BADMINTON / A FRIENDLY MATCH
Top right	—
Lower left	M. Ellen Edwards in 'The Girl's Own Paper'
Lower right	1882

or

Top left	EVENTS IN AFRICA // ZULU WAR / DEATH OF THE PRINCE IMPERIAL
Top right	1879
Lower left	Caton Woodville in the 'Illustrated London News'
Lower right	—

These represent just the usages employed at one particular picture library, with a particular type of material and catering for a particular type of user. Circumstances may require a different library, with different material and different usership, to adopt quite a different approach. But what is important is that the system should be convenient both to the staff and to the user, and should be designed to eliminate as much work as possible.

Cross-references
You have a picture showing frozen meat being unloaded from an Australian ship at the London docks. If your library makes a speciality of refrigeration, or food, or transport, or trade, you will have no problem filing it. But if, as is more likely, it is a general collection, then you will have to decide between three courses of action:

a) Put it in the most likely file (if you can decide on it) and trust that if people are looking for such a picture and fail to find it in any of the other files, they will come to this one for it. This is the coward's way out.

b) Make additional copies of it, and place a copy in each of the appropriate files. This is clearly the best course of action; unfortunately, it is also the most expensive and the most time-consuming.

c) Put the picture itself in one file, and put cross-references to it in any other place that is appropriate.

Cross-referencing should be a continuous and on-going process at all times. It can take many forms. The most economical is to place a special card—preferably of a contrasting colour—in every file where the situation arises, bearing the words 'SEE ALSO. . .' On this card you write, as they arise, indications as to where other material is to be found that could be relevant. Sometimes it will be to a general file: thus, under RIDING the reference card might suggest the user also looks at HUNTING, RACING and MILITARY / CAVALRY. Other references will be to specific pictures: thus, again under RIDING, you might be invited to look at a certain portrait showing Charles I or Cromwell on horseback.

Another helpful form of cross-referencing is to have a file dedicated entirely to cross-reference cards for awkward subjects which the user might not at first thought find it easy to locate. For instance:

Gates
Sun dials
Weather vanes
Sponge fishing
UFOs
Gipsies
Servants

Others will undoubtedly arise in the course of the daily round. The important thing is to make a note of requests that puzzle user and/or staff, and stop the gap with the help of a reference card.

Reference cards will also be required directing the user to material which for one reason or another cannot be filed in the main collection, either because it is too large, or too fragile, or too valuable. It may also be helpful to insert a reference in the black-and-white files when there is colour material in the transparency collection on the same subject.

Additional references should also be made to material kept in books and periodicals. Ideally, every book or other non-fileable item should be indexed and cross-referenced; unfortunately, like most ideals, this is quite impracticable. Even if a member of your staff were to sit down and work his way through the *Illustrated London news* from the year dot to the present, making a note of every picture, the chances are that he would miss certain aspects of some of the pictures —which would inevitably turn out to be just the aspect for which some visitor is hunting. How could any degree of indexing meet the needs of one researcher who asked a London picture library for pictures which depicted the influence of wars on hair styles?

Nonetheless, simply because a project is ultimately un-realisable does not mean that it should not be attempted; for this is one of those cases where even a partly-done job is better than none at all. If the staff are trained to make a note, as they flip through the pages of a book for a particular item, to keep an eye open for any other interesting items, this will little by little build up into a valuable back-up reference tool.

Cataloguing

In a book library a catalogue is essential; in a picture library this is not necessarily the case.

Ideally, yes, a catalogue is a nice thing to have, with each picture listed as it is added to the collection, on an index card or in a book, with its title if it has one, its artist if known, its source and date, and of course its subject matter. And, since we are talking of ideals, and because when it comes to pictures a verbal description is inadequate to convey the contents of a picture, a visual reference in the form of a miniature reproduction is desirable. If the visitor to a book library is seeking a book entitled *Oliver Twist*, and you happen to have a book with that title on your shelves, the chances are you have the book he wants; but if he wants a picture of the Taj Mahal, you may have a dozen pictures of the Taj Mahal and still not have the particular one he is looking for.

There are certain types of picture collections for which an index is not only feasible, but positively essential. These are for the most part homogeneous collections, where a researcher is likely to be seeking a particular item among a number of similar items—for example, a collection of ship plans, or architectural drawings, or photographs of stately homes. A simple list of what the collection contains will save everyone a lot of time and trouble.

But not always. Suppose the researcher is looking, not so much for a particular ship plan, but for examples of ship plans made by a particular naval architect? You will need an index by architects to supplement the straightforward catalogue which will presumably be by names of ships. And what if he is looking, not for views of stately homes by name, but for those which show conservatories or ha-has? Only a visual reference will save you thousands of man-hours of exhaustive cataloguing in which every possible item is painstakingly enumerated. And even then there is the possibility that the indexer will forget to note which views show topiary-work, or French windows, or croquet lawns. . .

In short, it all boils down yet again, to the question of what kind of pictures you have and what sort of users you get. How sophisticated would a catalogue have to be to cater for their needs; how much staff time and labour would it take to create such a catalogue; and would such effort be justified by the use made of it?

Judged by such a criterion many—perhaps most—picture libraries would decide that a catalogue of individual items was impracticable, at any rate for the greater part of their collection. For, in a sense, if the material is arranged along the lines described in this book, the pictures do largely form their own catalogue. It may not be quite so convenient to flip through large mounted pictures as small index cards, but at least there is the knowledge that once an item is located, what the user has is not merely a direction where to find the item, but the item itself.

A viable alternative procedure is to maintain a subject catalogue. This would not set out to list every individual picture, but would direct the user to the various parts of the library where material relating to that subject is to be found. Thus, needing pictures relating to the British General Strike of 1926, he might find a card saying:

GENERAL STRIKE 1926
Main file : EVENTS IN BRITAIN 1926
Secondary file : Newspaper ephemera (original copies)
                   Also available on microfilm.
Transparency file : EVENTS IN BRITAIN 1926
See also : *Illustrated London news, Punch*

However, even this degree of cataloguing is not necessary if the cross-reference policy described in the previous section is adopted. For this provides for just the type of secondary direction that would be contained in a catalogue, without the necessity for a separate index in book or file-card form. The great majority of subjects would be found in the logical place in the library, with cross-reference cards indicating that additional material is to be found elsewhere. And with regard to the awkward subjects which elude everyday logic, these can, as already suggested, be treated to individual reference cards, in some easily accessible place which is, nevertheless, compatible with the main collection.

The Anglo-American cataloguing rules: British text (Library Association, 1967) dealt much more fully with prints, paintings, drawings, photographs and transparencies, than does the recent AACR2.

The introduction to chapter fifteen of AACR1—*Pictures, designs and other two-dimensional reproductions*—explains that the rules detailed in the chapter, covering single works, sets of works and collections, 'are designed for standard catalogue entries, which may be integrated with other entries in a general library catalogue.'

However, from our point of view—that of the librarian of a picture library—we endorse another statement in the introduction: '. . . most pictorial works collected by libraries may be economically and efficiently serviced by arrangement in files by subject or other category. . .'

That is what we have attempted to demonstrate throughout this chapter.

SIX

LENDING AND COPYING

A LIMITED number of those who make use of picture libraries wish simply to have sight of a picture, mutter a disappointed oh, or an appreciative ah, and then return it to the files, satisfied. The majority, however, have some ulterior purpose in mind, and to achieve that purpose it is frequently necessary for them to have possession either of the picture or of a copy of it.

Principles
The purposes for which users may require the picture vary considerably, and it will certainly be the case that not all the varied uses to which users would like to put pictures are acceptable to all libraries. Consequently, a librarian should be well aware of what uses others might wish to put his pictures to, and be clear in his mind whether he is willing to approve them. If he decides to place any restrictions on those uses, then this should be clearly stated to clients before they make any attempt to use the library's facilities, in order not to waste their time nor the library's. For example, some collections will not permit their material to be used for advertising purposes. Again, some art collections are willing that their pictures may be used, but only if reproduced *in toto*, and in conformity with a specified level of quality.

Probably the most frequent type of use made of pictures in picture libraries is for reproduction in a book, periodical, television programme or audio-visual presentation. For this purpose, either the picture or a copy of it must be sent to the printer (for convenience' sake let us use the word 'printer' to stand for all those technicians who process the picture for the various picture-using media) and he will then make the

91

necessary 'artwork' in the form of a printing block, plate or other intermediary. In principle, this can be done without in any way affecting the picture itself; in practice, it is more frequent than otherwise for printers to make marks on the picture or its mount, sometimes eradicable and sometimes not. For this reason it is uncommon for picture libraries to allow their original material to be used for reproduction purposes, unless it is of relatively little value, when they can face the prospect of its loss or damage with equanimity. Sometimes, however, there will be cases where the picture will lose so much of its quality by being copied that the library will permit its original to be borrowed for reproduction purposes, but on strict conditions and with appropriate safeguards. In any case, it should always be made clear from the start that any loss or damage must be paid for, though this does not generally act as a deterrent to the printers, who as a class are deplorably indifferent to the products of their trade.

The decision as to whether to lend pictures at all and, if willing to do so, whether to lend the original or require the user to purchase a copy, is one on which practice varies widely from one library to another. Here, as in so many other respects of picture librarianship, there is no single preferred procedure because so much depends on the nature and value of the material and the type of user the library exists to serve. The options are:

a) to lend the original.

b) to lend a photographic copy of the original made by the library.

c) to sell a photographic copy of the original made by the library.

d) to allow the user, or a photographer appointed by the user or specified by the library, to make his own photographic copy of the original.

Which of these options is in fact selected will depend on the factors mentioned above, but will in practice largely differ according as to whether the picture library's material is: photographic; non-photographic and valuable; non-photographic and not especially valuable. (Many libraries, of course, will have material from all three categories, in which case it is likely that their procedure will vary according to the category of the material.)

If a library has photographic material, then it will normally require users to purchase copyprints of its photographs, since these cost relatively little—certainly not enough to justify the expense of setting up a loan system in all its complexity. Thus a press agency will not usually lend material, but will meet users' needs by providing them with a copyprint of the item they require, which they will purchase and which will become their property; though, as we shall see, this does not give them unlimited right to use that item.

If a library has valuable non-photographic material, it will not, of course, be willing to allow those items to leave the library; consequently, it will institute some form of copying procedure.

If a library has non-photographic material of no great value, it may feel that the best way it can serve its users is by allowing that material to be borrowed, albeit on specific conditions. In practice, most picture libraries which see their primary function as providing a service to a particular public, will adopt some form of loan procedure; though they will generally offer copy-and-purchase as an alternative for those users who find it more convenient.

Loan procedures

Because most users need a picture only temporarily, they for the most part have no wish to be involved in more expense than they have to; consequently, they would prefer to borrow material rather than purchase it. Most picture libraries which possess material suitable for loaning will, therefore, institute some form of loan procedure. It is, however, a complex process; and it is essential that the machinery for lending pictures should be carefully planned from the outset so as to meet all possible contingencies—of which, of course, the chief one is making sure the library gets its pictures back again, and in good condition.

These are some of the factors which the procedural system must take into account:

a) The library will require some kind of assurance that the user can be trusted with the material, that he will look after it and return it when he has finished with it. For this, some kind of authority may be required from his employer, director of studies or whatever.

b) The library will require a record of his name, address and telephone number so that it can contact him to know why the material has not been returned and so forth. This will entail conscientious record-keeping.

c) The library will need to know the purpose for which the item is being borrowed, to ensure that this is acceptable.

d) The library must keep a strict record of what material has been loaned, and over what period. It will probably wish to set a time limit for the period during which the picture may be retained, and may wish to impose a fine system should the picture be retained beyond that limit.

Much of this is, of course, comparable to the procedures of any type of lending library, but there are crucial differences. The first of these is that, while books are generally borrowed solely to be read or studied and returned, with pictures some ulterior objective is generally intended. This will almost certainly involve on-loaning to photographers, printers, editors, producers, and other individuals unknown to the library and whose dependability is indeed likely largely to be beyond the control of the person who actually borrows the material—even though they will, naturally, be held responsible for any loss or damage. Consequently, loaned pictures are very much more at risk than loaned books are likely to be. In any case, pictures themselves are more vulnerable physically.

There is also the factor that pictures are only rarely loaned one at a time: it is customary for the picture researcher, who needs a picture of lion hunting in Africa, to take away a selection of pictures on the subject so that his editor or some other person may select the one most appropriate for the actual need. This, again, involves further complication; for it may well be that the researcher, once the decision has been made, will return all but one of the pictures, or will start by weeding out the obviously unsuitable and returning those,

94

keeping a short list of possible candidates which will again be returned in instalments. The library's procedural methods have got to be able to handle this sort of thing.

Finally, there is the possibility that the library will want to make a charge for the use of its services and/or material, as we shall be considering in the next chapter. If this is the case, then the necessity for strict control, and a record of each stage in the transaction, will be vital to avoid arguments.

To ensure that the loaning procedure achieves its end despite these complexities, it will need to comprise the following items or their equivalent:

A card index should be maintained, with an individual card for each individual user, carrying:

his name, address and telephone number

his employer or other authority to whom recourse can be made should he disappear, defect or default

a reference to each transaction in which he is involved with the library

A slip or card should be made for each loan operation, carrying the following details:

A transaction or job number, one for each transaction, which must appear on every document or note relating to the transaction, and which will provide the reference on the user's card mentioned above so that reference can be made from that card to this job slip if more complete information is required.

The name and identifying data for the user (no need to note the address etc, as this is on his card).

The date of the transaction.

Indication of the nature of the material.

Number of items borrowed.

Purpose for which borrowed.

Provision for noting the number and date of return, bearing in mind that pictures may be returned sporadically. One way of doing this is to have the numbers 1 to 100 printed on the slip, which can be crossed out as the pictures are returned; but this involves individual numbering of the pictures, which may not be the method most suitable for the library.

Name of the staff member responsible for the transaction.

It is normal practice to supply a duplicate of this slip, bearing all or some of the data, to the individual borrowing the material, so that he too has a record of the transaction. On this document, generally described as a 'delivery note', the library may well wish to set out the conditions, or the more important of them, on which the material is loaned.

If the library has set a time limit for the loan, it must be prepared to chase the borrower after that time limit has expired. Consequently the job slips (or whatever you choose to call them) must be filed in such a way as to facilitate such automatic chasing.

Also on the job slip will be any specific information—for instance, if the loan period has been extended because of special circumstances, if a fee has been negotiated, or any other special observations. This, consequently, becomes the supreme source of information relating to the individual transaction, to which reference can be made from any other document.

To the librarian setting up a loan procedural system for the first time, all this will, doubtless, sound somewhat daunting. Unfortunately, it really is necessary. A slipshod system, which seeks to evade involving the staff in these complexities, will result ultimately in *more* work, *more* trouble for the staff and *more* one-off decision-making. It is absolutely essential to initiate an all-embracing and water-tight loan procedure right from the start, and operate it rigorously and conscientiously, if the staff are to be spared sorting out muddles in the future.

Copying by the library
Even a library which is willing to loan its material will almost certainly need to copy some or all of the material it loans. This may be for various reasons: some of its material may be too valuable, too fragile or too large to be loaned; there may be a chance that others will wish to use the same item, so it is desirable that a duplicate should be available; or, a user may wish for a copy of an item in a book or periodical.

A library which is geared to making its material available

for users, in any form or to any degree, will need to have arrangements for copying material. This may take the form of employing an outside photographer, on some kind of regular basis. Sometimes the photographer will come in once a week, or as necessary, and copy a batch of material; sometimes he will be paid by the library, sometimes he will be paid by the user who asks for the picture to be copied.

It is, of course, more convenient if the library can set up its own photographic department. If there is any substantial flow of copying work this is almost certainly the most economical in the long run. There will be a relatively heavy initial investment in equipment; but, thereafter, costs can be kept far lower than it is economical for an outside photographer to charge. And there are other advantages stemming from the fact that the whole operation is entirely under the control of the library, starting with the obvious one that the photographic files can be more readily integrated with the rest of the library.

Whether or not the photographs are made by his own photographic department or by an outsider, will not make very much difference to the policy the librarian adopts with regard to copying. This will stem directly from his needs. He may choose to copy some of his material on a speculative basis when, for instance, he comes across an interesting item in a periodical knowing that it will be asked for sooner or later, and it would be advantageous to have it ready copied rather than start the whole process when the time comes. This will apply in particular to those picture libraries which provide the sort of service which caters to picture researchers who need their material immediately; but, of course, it involves a certain amount of investment, and the financial arrangements of the library may be such that such anticipatory copying is not viable. Consequently, the majority of copying will always be done as the result of a specific request from a user.

The librarian then has the choice whether to loan or to sell the resulting copyprint, and if so, at what price—in other words, is the user who has commissioned the copying of the picture to be required to pay the cost of *making* the photograph—that is, including the negative cost—or only for the print?

If the user pays for making the negative, which will nearly always be retained by the library, then the library will profit because, should another user come along and ask to use the same picture and purchase a copyprint, it will not have to be re-photographed. (The librarian can then decide whether to charge the second user the full cost of photography as a standard charge, irrespective of whether it has previously been photographed or not, and thus make a modest profit for the library, or give the benefit of the earlier photography to the second user, who will thus pay much less than his predecessor, which seems unfair. . .)

Alternatively, a library may be anxious to build up its negative files, and be perfectly happy to bear the cost of making a photograph, charging the user only for the cost of the print, if the print is sold, or nothing at all if it is loaned.

The reader is warned that this is a complex and many-faceted aspect of picture librarianship. It may help to note three examples of how such approaches work out in practice, derived from three London picture libraries:

The National Portrait Gallery is keen that all its original material should be photographed. So if a user asks for a copyprint of a paritcular picture, he has to pay only for that print, not for making the negative.

The Saint Bride Printing Library cannot carry the cost of photographing, at public expense, its vast collection of specialist material. If a picture has been photographed previously, the user simply pays the cost of making a further copyprint. But if it has not previously been photographed, then he must pay for the cost of making the negative also.

The Mary Evans Picture Library sees it as part of its service to its clients to make any of its material available in a usable from, and to this end is willing to itself pay the cost of making a copyprint of any item which cannot be loaned as it is. Should the user wish to retain the copy, of course, then he must pay for it, but normally copied pictures are supplied on a loan basis. The only exception is when a client requests a copy of some very obscure item which the library would not

98

wish to give space to in its files, in which case the user is required to pay the full cost.

Copying by the user
Many picture libraries have no photographic facilities of their own and do not wish to get involved in that side of the subject; some even carry this reluctance to the extent of being unwilling to have an outside photographer come in to make copies on request. They prefer that users wishing for copies of their material should make their own arrangements, sending in a photographer by arrangement, or taking it themselves. This was formerly normal practice at many major museums, though it is slowly disappearing as these institutions make their own arrangements.

When such a facility is granted, it is frequently the case that the library will charge an access or disturbance fee. The negative of any picture so copied remains the property of the photographer. It should be made clear to all concerned that the act of taking the photograph does not give the photographer or the user any right to use the picture in any public fashion until permission has been obtained from the owner of the original. (The extremely complicated subject is considered more fully in the section on copyright.)

Copying equipment
The technical aspects of copying pictures are quite complex enough to fill a book on their own, and will appear daunting to the librarian who does not happen also to be an experienced photographer. However, there are many types of equipment on the market today which can be used by someone who is in no way an expert, which can be a tremendous convenience to the library and save a very substantial sum of money.

Photostat machine
A machine which produces photostats (often called photocopies, but this term should be avoided not only because it is strictly inaccurate but also because it is misleading and apt to create confusion) is an indispensable tool which every library should possess. If the volume of use justifies it, the Xerox machine is unquestionably the best; but, for simply

99

financial reasons, most libraries will choose one of the more modest—and modest-priced—appliances available. There are many of them and when making your choice the following criteria are relevant:

a) Do not be tempted to get a small table-top machine. They give poor results and are very liable to breakdown.

b) A 'dry' process is in general to be preferred to a 'wet' one, particularly if it prints on to ordinary paper compared with the rather distasteful coated kind. However, most dry-copy machines tend to be more expensive than the wet type and to be less practicable in use, so do not be surprised if you end by finding this criterion has to be ignored.

c) A stat machine for library use should be of the 'flat' rather than the rotary design, as this enables books and rigid cards to be copied as well as flimsy items.

d) If possible, the design should be one in which it is the light which travels, rather than the item being copied, as this will save the handling of books and other awkward objects.

e) A design which uses a continuous roll of paper is to be preferred to one which uses individual sheets of paper. It causes fewer paper-jams—the most common cause of break-down—and also means that the size of the copy can be adjusted to match that of the item, which is convenient as well as economical.

f) Other things being equal, obtain the most robust model, and the one which requires fewest adjustments on the part of the user, for it is likely that it will often be used by people who are clumsy or not fully conversant with its use.

Once you have installed your stat machine you will have to work out a policy for it, such as who is to use it—one particular member of the staff, all the staff, or staff and visitors—and whether a charge is to be made for its use.

More crucial decisions will have to be made regarding the functions the photostat machine is to perform in the library context. There will inevitably be many of the usual everyday jobs—copying letters and other documents, information from books, pages from bibliographies and the like. But, of course, in a picture library there are many—perhaps countless—ways in which a stat machine can make library functioning easier, by enabling visual references to be provided instead of verbal descriptions. Common sense will suggest many of these, and experience will add many more. Most of them will boil down to variations on the case where a user of the library, wishing to know what visual material is available on a given subject, can take away or be sent a collection of stats instead of the material itself.

It must always be remembered that pictures, and books containing pictures, can very easily be damaged in the course of making a photostat, particularly if the machine is of a kind where the original being copied moves in relation to the light source. For this reason, the job, trivial though it is, should not be entrusted to an inexperienced member of the staff, and the visitor should never be allowed to make his own copies unless he is known to be familiar with the machine and trustworthy with the material.

Black and white photography
Although it is the most common form of professional photography, black and white photography remains also the most complex. Unless there is a trained photographer on the library staff, or the library can afford to hire one to come in either full-time or for a regular period every week, it is probably best to pass all black and white copying to a professional outsider, perhaps on a retainer basis.

Although there are as yet no proper short-cuts to effective black and white photography, there are two types of appliance on the market which can prove useful to a picture library. Both can be used by anyone, whether or not he has any photographic experience.

Polaroid. This manufacturer markets an integrated system which can be housed on a (large) table top, tucked away in a corner of the library, and does not require dark room conditions. It will provide copyprints of any type of material, of very high quality and perfectly suitable for reproduction. The one drawback is that the pictures are only 12 x 9 cm in size, but against this is the fact that they can be produced instantly—that is, in less than two minutes.

It is possible by using a different type of film to produce
101

a negative by this process; and from this negative, of course, copyprints of any size can be made. To do this, however, more sophisticated facilities are required, including darkroom conditions for the printing process, which somewhat does away with the convenience of the basic system.

By using various additional equipment, the Polaroid system can be extended to meet many interesting applications. One of these enables 25 x 20 cm colour prints to be made, of magnificent quality and at a price which compares very favourably with that of professional copying. Certain types of library might well find this useful.

PMT (Photo Mechanical Transfer) Machine: This consists of a free-standing 'camera' some two metres high and one metre square. It requires darkroom conditions, but in all other respects is very convenient and undemanding—for instance, no water supply is required.

The PMT is a highly versatile machine, but for picture libraries its most important application will be its ability to make copies of illustrations, especially line illustrations, of very high quality—suitable for reproduction—in about two minutes. Pictures can be enlarged or reduced, combined or masked; pictures can be in books or periodicals, and of almost any size up to that of a newspaper page.

It must be confessed that the quality when copying photographs and other continuous-tone items is not always satisfactory, and it cannot at this stage of development be recommended for this purpose, though sometimes results can be excellent. But when it is a matter of line work—for instance, a Bewick woodcut or an illustration from a Victorian periodical—the quality is astonishingly good. At least two historical picture libraries in Britain use the machine and find it amply justifies a cost which, with ancillary equipment, is currently (1980) somewhat over £1000.

Colour transparencies
It is easy to fail to recognise the fact that colour photography, where a transparency is the end product, is actually a simpler process than black and white photography, because it is a

one-stage process—the processed film becomes the transparency—whereas black and white photography is a two-stage process which requires prints to be made from the negative.

It is, in fact, remarkably easy to make your own colour transparencies, even though no member of the staff has any professional experience and though there are no darkroom facilities. A simple set-up can be installed, with a camera on a stand: because most of the items to be copied will be of much the same type (compared with normal photography where the subject matter is apt to vary from a distant landscape to an interior close-up of the family round the Christmas tree) simple guidelines can be set-up so that the copying process is almost automatic. In a very short while transparencies can be produced at a cost which is only a fraction of that charged by professionals, and the quality can be just as high. The film is, of course, sent off to a processing laboratory for processing. These days, this is a very simple matter, and the films can often be processed in two or three hours so that the entire procedure is completed within the day.

It is not the purpose of this chapter to do more than indicate some of the ways in which a picture library can make its life much easier by exploring the possibilities of doing its own picture copying. This is a field where a very great deal of technological improvement is taking place all the time, and even as this is being written, new developments are probably on the way which will give the library even greater ability to control its own copying. The best course is to establish a good relationship with a convenient photographic store—you will need to get your supplies from somewhere, after all—and consult them about the choice of equipment, given your specific needs.

SEVEN

MAKING A CHARGE FOR SERVICES

A GOOD deal has been said already in this book concerning the responsibility of the library towards those it was created to serve and this must, indeed, affect the conduct and procedure of the library in every detail and ramification of its work. The way in which that responsibility is translated into practice will dictate not only the broad lines along which the library is set up, and its material acquired and made available, but also secondary questions as to what back-up facilities and services shall be provided for the convenience of users.

General principles
Many of these facilities represent a departure from the fundamental concept of a library as a place for storage and reference. For example, it is rare for a book library to provide facilities for books to be copied; at most, there may be photostat facilities providing for cheap low-quality copies of individual pages, suitable only for verbal reference. In a picture library, by contrast, it is more often than not the practice to provide facilities whereby copies of its pictures, of a suitable quality for reproduction, can be made available by one means or another.

To provide such facilities is obviously expensive, both in the initial investment in the necessary equipment, and in the running costs, including the material supplies required and the additional staff time demanded. Sometimes these additional costs will be absorbed by the library budget; for example where the services of the picture library are regarded as a function of some such establishment as an art college. But even in such cases, it is doubtful if the administration will want to go beyond a certain limited point in providing such services gratis. Consequently, to almost every librarian there comes, sooner or later, a time for deciding just what he is prepared to do, and on what terms, to provide users with copies of his material.

The answer will, of course, be prejudged if the library is a commercial one, whose sole source of income consists of the fees derived from making its material available for reproduction. In such a case, a scale of fees will be worked out for the various services provided, and these will be offered to the public along straightforward cost-effective lines, and the library will sink or swim according to its ability to offer the user the material and services he requires at a viable cost.

But with non-commercial picture libraries, the situation is fraught with moral issues for the librarian. His library exists to serve the—or at any rate a—public: how is this to be reconciled with levying charges? The dilemma is particularly acute when the library is maintained by public funds. In such cases, there is a tendency to believe that anyone who uses the library has a right to make whatever use he wishes of its services without paying a penny.

A moment's reflection will reveal the naiveté of such a viewpoint; nevertheless, the dilemma remains and the librarian and his governing body must decide whether those services shall be provided free of charge, or at a subsidised rate, or at the full market rate. In practice, this means deciding either to provide what is possible within the budget limits; or to provide a basic minimum service free of charge and, thereafter, to charge for any additional services.

If they opt for the second of these alternatives, they must further decide whether to charge for these services at cost price, or to make a modest profit, and use this to increase the services and improve the facilities of the library.

That word 'profit' is, of course, a red rag to many librarians; there has been a long-raging controversy about this matter in the library world and, no doubt, it will long continue to rage. The fact that librarians are so concerned about the matter is a reflection of their integrity and a measure of their determination to serve their public. Nevertheless, it is fair to point out that serving one section over-generously can be done only at the expense of other members of the public.

106

For, sooner or later, *somebody* has to pay for those services; it becomes a question of who that somebody should be.

The profit yardstick
If that word 'profit' is faced coolly and logically, it will be seen that there is in fact a simple yardstick whereby the librarian can make a fair decision. It is this: are the facilities provided by the library being used by the user for his financial advantage, or simply in the course of his educational or professional work or duties?

A simple, everyday example is when pictures are being borrowed by a researcher on behalf of a publisher who will eventually be selling the book, containing reproductions of the library's pictures, as a commercial proposition. If this is the case, the publisher is deriving a benefit from the services and, unless he pays a fair return for that benefit, he is obtaining it at the expense of those who provide the services; which in most cases is the taxpayer or the ratespayer—that is, the other possible users of the library.

Consequently, it is only fair that such a user should be required to pay a reasonable fee for the use of the material, at least sufficient to cover the cost of providing the service. If this logic is accepted, then the librarian simply has to make the basic decision, will his library make its material freely available to users who wish to exploit it for their own commercial advantage. If it will, then it must take the consequences.

Charging reproduction fees
Once you decide that the library will formally charge for the reproduction of its material, the necessary administration machinery must be set up just as it was when the library decided that it would loan its material. Here, too, it is essential that a comprehensive procedural system be devised from the outset, capable of coping with all contingencies, in order to save time, trouble and argument later.

Basically, the question of charging for the use of material consists of deciding what to charge, asking for the money, and saying thank you when you get it. In practice, however, there are some complicating factors:

a) Records must be kept of all transactions, to satisfy your accountants and in case of subsequent dispute. The requisite paperwork can in practice be dovetailed with that required for the lending out and checking in of loaned material, but will need to be carefully planned so that information on any on-going transaction is immediately to hand.

b) Rates charged for the reproduction of illustrated material vary according to the type of use. Considerably more is charged when a picture is used on the front jacket of an international best-seller, than when the same picture is used in the charity programme of the local musical society's annual concert. It may seem to be making things easier to have a flat rate for all types of use, but this will result either in being unnecessarily hard on the local singers, or unnecessarily generous to the international publisher. Consequently most picture libraries have a sliding scale of rates, sometimes —in the case of libraries which cater for a wide range of usership—extremely complicated in order to take into account all contingencies. But once such a rates structure has been established, it eliminates a great deal of one-off decision-making, which is tedious and exhausting.

c) Most publishers do not expect to pay for the use of pictures until the book or periodical in which it appears is formally published. There will, therefore, be a considerable interval between the date of borrowing and the date when payment is made for the use of the material. Some picture libraries refuse to accept this, and if they carry sufficient clout, are able to insist that publishers pay in advance before the material is made available to them. The disadvantage of this is that researchers cannot always be sure, when they make their initial selection, that the items will be definitely used. To pay in advance for an item which may not be used is clearly a cumbersome arrangement, even if provision is made for the refund of the money should the picture not eventually be used. Consequently, this method is usually used only by picture libraries which do not loan their material, but make copies which the user has to purchase. What happens then is that the researcher takes some kind of reference—perhaps a photostat—of the item, and orders a print only when he knows that it will certainly be used.

It is important to keep in mind that what the user is paying for is the *service* rendered by the library—the making available of the material in a form that he can use. The fee, therefore, has no relation to the picture itself, its value or original cost. This is not an easy point to explain to a user who wonders why he should pay £10 to reproduce a picture which cannot have cost as much as that to purchase. But somehow he must be made to realise that what he is paying for is the acquisition and identification of the material; its cleaning, mounting and captioning; its filing and cataloguing; the lighting and heating and humidification requisite for suitable and convenient storage and access; the staff time and labour involved in loaning the item and checking it back; and all the concomitant paperwork. The user is, in fact, obtaining a professional service, albeit provided by a public institution, and it is that service he is paying for.

Setting the rate
Given that the rate at which a user is charged for making use of the library's pictures is in return for a specific service, it follows that it will vary according to the quality of that service. Consequently, rates charged for the reproduction of pictures varies widely. A glossy news agency, employing some of the world's finest photographers, and making their material available instantly and unconditionally, is clearly entitled to charge—and most assuredly does charge—more than a private individual who is unable to provide such facilities and whose work is not of a comparable quality. The *British Association of Picture Libraries and Agents* (BAPLA), though not legally permitted to set a fixed rate, issues guidelines for commercial sources which are adhered to, more or less, by most established picture libraries in Britain; and other countries have their equivalents. There are similar organisations for individual photographers, fashion photographers and other specialist categories.

It should not be forgotten, moreover, that the cost of retrieving reproduction fees has itself to be built into those fees. Consequently, they must be set at a realistic level, and be reassessed in the light of rising prices, wages etc. It is actually more economical to charge no fee at all, and avoid the associated work, than to charge too low a fee and find that the fee retrieval system is actually costing you more than the revenue it brings in.

The rates charged by such BAPLA members are generally higher than those charged by the majority of picture libraries, particularly those which are administered by public authorities or professional bodies. The *Museums Association* has set up guidelines for the guidance of public collections in this matter, with rates running at approximately fifty per cent of those suggested by BAPLA for commercial sources. This would seem to be a realistic level in view of the fact that the facilities of public picture libraries are at least partially subsidised by the ratespayer or taxpayer, whereas the commerical library is probably wholly dependent on income from reproduction fees. In general, it may be said—without any intention of blame or disapproval—that public picture libraries do not offer the user the same standard of service as that provided by commercial sources.

As to the complexity of the charges structure, this must be related to the type of user and the amount of use; but as already explained, there are good arguments in favour of being prepared for as many contingencies as possible. Here are the headings from a typical wide-ranging rates structure, simply as an indication of what the library must be prepared for:

Books—one country, additional countries, world;
    one edition only, several editions, translations;
    jackets, covers, endpapers;
    dummies, layouts.
Peridodicals—sold in one country, distributed in many
    countries;
    less than half page, less than page, whole page or over;
    national magazines, house journals, trade journals.
Television
Audio-visual
Advertising—press advertising;
    television commercials.
Miscellaneous
    exhibitions;

murals in offices, pubs;
calendars, greetings cards, non-commercial posters;
programmes, menus;
record sleeves etc.

Other fees
One phrase often leads to confusion, and that is the usage 'print fee' by which is meant, in fact, the material cost of supplying a photographic copyprint. Strictly speaking, this is not a fee at all, but a material purchase price.

Fees are charges for services rendered. The first and much the most important of these is for providing the picture for purposes of reproduction; this constitutes the reproduction fee which has already been discussed. There are also additional fees which may be charged at the library's discretion:

Service fee: This is a charge made when the library staff go to an inordinate amount of trouble to carry out the user's request—whether in the form of research, or in allowing a large number of pictures to be borrowed, or any such service. It is emphasised that this is not to be regarded as a source of revenue, but simply to cover the overheads involved in providing the service. Some picture libraries levy a nominal service fee to cover the costs of providing *any* requested material. This has the advantage that, supposing the user eventually decides not to make any use of the material, or only a very small use, the library will nonetheless be to some extent reimbursed for the cost of providing the material.

Holding fee: It is customary to fix a time limit for the retention of the loaned material by a user. After this date, as with a book library, they become liable to pay a fee unless an extension is requested and granted. Again, this should not be seen as a source of revenue, but in this case as a deterrent against holding material which might be of use to some other client.

EIGHT

COPYRIGHT

AS SOON as a picture library starts to make use of its pictures in any way, it is liable to become involved in the question of copyright. It seems appropriate, therefore, to give a general outline of the matter; though what follows should be taken only as a guide and not as a comprehensive and definitive statement of this extremely complex subject.

Copyright defined
Copyright is the right of the copyright holder to give or withhold permission for his picture to be reproduced.

The copyright holder is not necessarily the person who owns the picture, for the owner may have assigned the copyright to some other person or institution. Equally, the copyright holder need not be the person who created the picture; again, the artist or photographer may have assigned the right to his heirs in case of his death, or to his employer by contract if, for example, he is employed to take photographs on behalf of a periodical.

In other words, copyright is an abstract right, unaffected by ownership or possession of the item to which it refers.

Copyright and reproduction right
If a library possesses a picture, it does not necessarily follow that it also owns the copyright in that picture, unless this has been specifically assigned to it. If it possesses a picture which is still in copyright (defined below) it is its responsibility to determine what the copyright position is and to act accordingly. If it is intended to make the picture available to users of the library for purposes of reproduction, then it must either establish that it owns the copyright, or that the

113

copyright owner is willing that the picture should be so used. In the latter case, it must be determined whether the copyright holder is willing to waive his right over the picture, or requires each person wishing to reproduce the picture to make specific application to him.

Thus it comes about that when a library makes a picture available for reproduction, it may in some cases allow the user to go ahead without further complication, while in others it requires the user to obtain copyright permission from the copyright holder. In the latter case it may refuse to supply the picture, or a copy of it, to the user until such permission has been obtained in writing.

The copyright holder, while able to give or withhold permission for the picture to be reproduced, may not be in a position to provide the would-be user with the picture or a copy of it. The owner of the picture, while unable to grant copyright, is in a position to give or withhold permission for the picture to be used simply because he has physical possession of the picture. Consequently, a second right exists, the reproduction right. This is not strictly a legal right in the same sense as copyright, but is only a special version of the normal property right which grants any of us the right to do as we wish with what is ours. Indeed, the owner of a Rembrandt painting is perfectly within his rights if he chooses to destroy that painting; and if he chooses to destroy a painting which is in copyright, and happens not to own the copyright, there is nothing the copyright holder can do to prevent him.

But though a library thus owns a reproduction right over the material in its possession, irrespective of any copyright, it does not have such a right over any other copies of that material which may exist; in the case of an engraving, for example, just because it has one copy of a picture, it cannot prevent a user obtaining another copy from somewhere else and using that. But it *can* prevent a user from making unlimited use of a copy of one of its own pictures, by stipulating, when that copy is provided, that purchase of that copy does not imply that henceforward the purchaser can reproduce the item freely. This should however be made clear when the copy is supplied.

In and out of copyright
A work of art is described as being 'in copyright' for a specified period, which extends during the creator's lifetime and for a specified period after his death. In Britain, this period is generally fifty years after the end of the year in which the creator died; the period varies in other countries, and so does the system by which copyright is established. In Britain, copyright is automatic; whereas in the United States it has to be registered. The period is unaffected by whether the artist has assigned the copyright to some other person or institution.

There are, however, several exceptions. The most notable of these is when the work was commissioned by a publisher for reproduction in a periodical or book. In such a case, copyright expires fifty years after the end of the year in which the picture was first published.

The copyright of a commissioned photograph belongs to whoever commissioned the photograph. In this case there is a difference in procedure depending on the date when the photograph was made:

If made *before* 1 June 1957, copyright expires fifty years after the end of the year in which the photograph was *made*.

If made *on or after* 1 June 1957, copyright expires fifty years after the end of the year in which the picture was first *published.*.

A further exception occurs in the matter of portraits, which in Britain are subject to special legislation if they are commissioned for financial or other payment. In such a case, the person who commissions the portrait—not necessarily the sitter—holds the copyright. However, the duration of the copyright continues to be linked to the life of the artist, even though he has no other right in the item.

Copyright in practice
As will now be evident, copyright is a complex and troublesome business. It is a pity that all countries do not use the sound common-sense method of the United States, where copyright must be claimed and registered; whereupon, it is

granted for a period of twenty-eight years, after which it must be renewed, otherwise it falls into the public domain. Such a system means that the copyright situation as regards any individual item can quickly and unequivocally be established; if there is no indication of copyright being claimed, the owner of the material knows that he is free to go ahead and use the item.

However, in the absence of any such clear-cut situation, it is incumbent on the librarian to be aware of the copyright situation as regards each item in his possession if he intends to allow them to be made available for purposes of reproduction. When it is a question of old prints and engravings, and other historical items, there is, of course, no problem; all that is entailed is his own reproduction right. As regards material from journals more than fifty years old, he is generally safe in concluding that copyright has expired, though there is always the possibility that copyright will not have been assigned to the publisher but retained by the artist or photographer, so if he considers that this may be the case he will be well advised to check the situation.

When it comes to more recent material, he should either contact the copyright holder and endeavour to reach some kind of agreement with him, or require would-be users of the material to get in touch with the copyright holder and make their own agreement; of which, written evidence must be produced before the library will make the material available. In such cases he should state clearly, when making the material available for inspection by users, that he claims only reproduction right in the material and that the user will be required to clear the copyright.

When copyright cannot be traced
It will frequently happen that it is impossible to establish the copyright ownership of a picture—for instance, a photograph reproduced in a book or magazine of the 1950s, where no credit line is affixed. In such a case, the prudent librarian or user, if he wishes to play absolutely safe, will be well advised not to seek to use that picture.

On the other hand, it may be the only picture of that particular subject, in which case he may be willing to take a chance. If so, he will be well advised:

to insert an advertisement in an appropriate periodical, asking the copyright holder to identify himself; and
to print a disclaimer in the published work, stating that attempts have been made to establish the copyright position, but that such attempts have failed, and stating that an appropriate copyright fee will be paid to anyone who can substantiate his claim to own the copyright.

In theory the copyright holder can claim any sum he likes as a fee for using the material, and if a picture has been used without his permission he may charge any sum he likes. But if it can be shown that the user has made sincere efforts to trace the copyright holder, this will generally be taken as an indication that he was acting in good faith, and it should not be too difficult to come to an amicable arrangement in the event—not in itself very likely—of the copyright holder claiming his right.

NINE

ADMINISTRATION

IT SHOULD be sufficiently evident by now that a picture library differs in a great many and very significant ways from a book library. From this it follows that the people who are best suited to work in it will not necessarily be those best fitted for a book library.

However, this applies only to the superficial aspects of the work. Basically, librarianship is a state of mind: librarians are born, not made; and the person who is suited to one kind of library work will probably be able to adapt to another without too much *angst*. He must be tidy; he must be orderly; he must have an instinct for preserving valuable things combined with a missionary spirit in making the public aware of those things; and he must love the things themselves.

General
The qualities to look for, when selecting staff for a picture library will, therefore, be those which reflect this inner attitude. A lively mind, able to make rapid mental connections, is absolutely essential, so that if a visitor asks for a specific item, the member of staff will be able to translate that request into actual terms. Unfortunately, there is no formal qualification which will ensure that an individual has this ability. It will be necessary for the interviewer to make his own tests to establish that the interviewee possesses it over and above whatever formal qualifications he is able to offer.

Formal qualifications
There is sufficient overlap between working in a picture library and working in any other kind of library for a general

119

library training to be appropriate. At the same time, the differences should be borne in mind and, other things being equal, the applicant who shows a special ability when it comes to visual abilities should be chosen.

That sounds self-evident, but it must be explained that 'visual abilities' is not by any means the same thing as a training in subjects related to visual items. A knowledge of art history is undoubtedly an advantage in any picture librarian, but in itself it is no guarantee of the type of mind best suited to everyday administration of a picture collection; for art history is largely a matter of book learning and the study of aspects of art only distantly related to practicalities. To take just one example: the question of reproducibility is not one which arises to any great extent when studying the history of art, yet it is absolutely vital in practical picture librarianship. So, while training in art is undoubtedly to be regarded as an asset, it is no guarantee that the applicant is capable of adapting his scholarship to the requirements of a picture library; in some cases it could actually form a stumbling block by inhibiting the vulgarisation inherent in providing a public service at an economical price.

As much as anything else, general knowledge is called for, particularly if the library is itself a general one. In the course of a day the member of a picture library staff may be asked for a portrait of Queen Alexandra before her marriage, a view of London Bridge showing the morning commuter stream, a selection of pictures of ornate cooked dishes, two pictures of New York depicting how it changed between 1850 and 1950, an ornamental figure representing Comedy and Tradedy, a schooner-rigged yacht, building methods in the Middle Ages, Richard Nixon as President of the United States, a refrigerator of the 1930s, the parable of the Good Samaritan, refugees in the Spanish Civil War. . . The picture librarian must be able to switch his mind instantly from one of these topics to the next, to go straight to the appropriate file if there is one, and if not, to make an informed guess as to which files will be the most likely to reveal what is required. He must be able to answer questions from users intelligently—not that he will be expected to be an expert on every subject—and he *will* be expected to know where to look for the necessary information.

120

Such an ability is most likely to have been acquired as a result of a higher education course, and there can be little question that a university training will be the best guarantee of the kind of ability a picture library requires. The actual knowledge may be quite irrelevant, but the ability to hunt out information, which a university training should have instilled, will be the librarian's greatest asset.

Most institutional picture libraries will expect formal professional library qualifications. In Britain, these are now generally acquired as a result of full-time attendance at a school of librarianship to take a librarianships degree course or a postgraduate diploma course and, after suitable practical experience, to become chartered by the Library Association. Many library schools now include special notice of picture librarianship, either as an integral part of the course or as an extra. There are also sporadic courses, seminars and workshops in picture librarianship organised by various interested bodies such as the Art Libraries Society (ARLIS) and the Publishers Association, but there is no regular or formal training available.

The indications are clear that this is unlikely to be the case for much longer. Picture librarianship, like picture research, is rapidly growing in professionalism; and the creation of specific picture libraries, where formerly there was only a collection of pictures housed within a book library, is contributing to the build-up of a special category within librarianship which will inevitably generate its own corporate identity.

Training
Having acquired a promising recruit, the next step is to instruct him in the basics of picture librarianship. Assuming that he has some knowledge of librarianship in general, the first essential is to explain in what ways picture librarianship differs from other forms. Then will follow indoctrination into:

a) How this particular library works—the overall procedure, and the minutiae of day to day operation. If this has been properly planned, the operation, though complex, should contain its own logic, so that at each point the question to be asked will not be 'what happens next?' but 'how do you do such-and-such?' Even though eventually each staff member will have his own individual role, it is essential that all should have a general awareness of all the various processes, so that in case of emergency each should be able to step into another's shoes. Naturally every library will have its own approach to its daily functioning, but wherever possible a rigid insistence on job compartmentalisation, particularly of a hierarchical nature, should be avoided—every member of the staff should be able, and not too unwilling, to turn his hand to filing or other dogsbody occupations if a bottleneck occurs.

b) The different types of pictures and the different ways they can be used. Even though he already has considerable knowledge of pictures *per se*, it must be emphasised that in picture library practice, different factors—such as the question of reproducibility already referred to—assume an importance of which the newcomer may not be aware.

c) The 'philosophy' of picture librarianship, so that he becomes aware of why this particular library functions the way it does, how it compares with other picture libraries, and what the user has a right to expect from this or any other picture library. He should also be informed as to alternative sources; so that if a visitor asks for help in a matter where this particular library is unable to assist, the staff member can direct him elsewhere, to a more specialist source, perhaps, or one offering different facilities more appropriate to his needs.

d) Public relations—the attitude adopted by the library as a whole towards its visitors, and how this translates into personal terms. This is an aspect which is easily overlooked, with results that are, to an outsider, only too evident in some cases; but it should be clear from what has been written earlier in this book that enormous differences exist between one library and another, and it is unfair on the user to expect him to be aware of those differences. The staff should, therefore, learn how to behave with regard to schoolchildren who want help with their projects; professional researchers making heavy demands with obscure requests; single-minded obsessives who would monopolise the staff's time if they could; and all the varied customers who come through the library door.

Most such indoctrination will be acquired as the result of on-the-spot daily experience, but there are various ways in which the new member of staff can be given the opportunity to learn more about his trade. He can be sent to visit museums and special exhibitions relevant to the subject matter of the library; he can be sent to visit a printing works to see how pictures are reproduced; he can be sent to visit the premises of those who use the library's pictures—publishers, television studios and the like—which will give him a better idea of the sort of material such users require; and he can be sent to visit other picture libraries, to compare their approach to the business with that of his own employer.

CASSELL'S

Working conditions
Pictures, even more than books, are fragile and vulnerable. They must be handled carefully, for wear and tear is probably the worst enemy they have to face. There is no point in giving them optimum storage conditions, if the conditions within which they are actually handled are inadequate—for it is at this point that they are in the greatest danger.

Consequently, the planning of the library must be designed with this in mind, and this means optimum working conditions for the staff, not only for their own sakes, but for that of the pictures for which they are responsible.

Space is the first criterion—space, and plenty of it. There should be provision of large empty flat surfaces at every possible point, so that pictures can be spread out rather than piled on top of each other. This means, amongst other things, that many objects which might otherwise occupy space, table, lamps, telephones, paper racks and tools such as rulers and so forth, should be housed either in wall fittings or in drawers, leaving a maximum of empty surface available.

Space is needed, too, in the vicinity of the picture storage facilities. This is, of course, especially true where large pictures are concerned—staff and users must not be expected to manoeuvre fragile items in confined spaces when, for instance, removing them from a plans chest. And if people are passing each other in aisles between furniture or walls, there should be plenty of room to pass so that pictures are not knocked or tilted with the possibility of slipping and falling.

But over and above these material considerations, space is important psychologically: the staff themselves must not feel confined, they should feel relaxed and able to stretch, for otherwise they will be too tense to handle the pictures with sufficient care.

Every effort should be made to ensure that the pictures are physically handled as little as possible; and when they are handled, then as gently as possible. Plastic trays, wallets and folders should be used to contain or carry pictures, rather than carrying them loose in the hand. See-through plastic folders should be used whenever appropriate, because then the item will not have to be removed from its container in order to be inspected. An enormous variety of such plastic stationery is available today, and parsimony in this respect is short-term economy. The generous availability of plastic containers of all kinds is the best way of encouraging staff to take proper care of the material.

It is, of course, essential that lighting should be of the best, for the more easily a picture can be seen, the less it will need to be physically handled. All the files and drawers should be under vertical illumination, and there should be spot lights for all tables and desks on which pictures are inspected or studied. Light-boxes should be readily available adjacent to the transparency files, together with magnifying glasses to enable details to be checked.

A well-selected library of reference books should be placed within easy access of the staff, and they should be encouraged to use them as much as possible, to familiarise themselves with the basic information sources. If a book is continually in demand, then it is sound sense to acquire another copy. For nothing will encourage staff to increase their own value to the library, and add to their own knowledge, better than giving them the opportunity to involve themselves in information-finding—we remember what we discover for ourselves far more than what others tell us.

Paperwork

Inevitably, picture librarianship, like any other librarianship, involves a considerable amount of tedious paperwork. Pictures need to be captioned, catalogue entries need to be made out, cross-references have to be indicated. On the administrative side, users' names and addresses must be taken and entered on card or in a book; each job must be individually recorded with all relevant dates; and details of loaned material must be kept, together with information about returned material and ultimate use. A note must be kept of charges, agreements and fees; photographers' orders must be entered in one place, orders to stationery suppliers in another; and so with each and every aspect of the daily running of the library. Much of this is only remotely connected with pictures *per se*, and is apt to be dismaying to the newcomer who has, perhaps, built up a rosy picture of a cultured existence devoted to the handling of pictures throughout the hours of the working day.

Some members of the staff will be recruited specifically to assist on the administrative side; and it is, fortunately, the case that there exist people whose propensities lie in this direction and who are actually happier with columns of figures than with pictures. Nevertheless, the whole of the staff will be to some extent involved in paperwork, and it is important that this should be fairly distributed.

Exhibitions

If your library contains valuable or interesting pictures, you may be asked to lend them for exhibition purposes. This raises several problems; some ethical, others merely practical.

In the first place, you will have to consider where your first loyalties lie—to your immediate usership, the people who come in person to visit your library, or to the community as a whole. For if you lend your pictures away for exhibition purposes. the chances are they will be away from the library for weeks at least, more probably months and, perhaps, especially if it is a touring exhibition, years. During that time, the normal users of the library will be denied access to them; and there is always the chance that they may never be seen again, due to loss or damage.

At the same time, if your library possesses unique material, or items which are uniquely accessible via your collection, this could be said to represent a trust you hold for humanity at large and, in a wider interest, you should enable the greatest possible number of people to see them; people who might not be able to visit, or might not think of visiting, your library for that purpose. This is particularly the case where the material you hold represents a vital element in the 'story' of the exhibition—a key picture, perhaps, in the career of a particular artist, or a landmark in the subject of the exhibition which cannot be adequately represented by a substitute.

Clearly, the decision whether or not to allow your material to be used for exhibition purposes is not one which can be made in accordance with general guidelines. All you can do is apply the foregoing criteria to the individual case.

If you do decide to allow your material to be used, you will of course lay down very strict conditions. These may include:

a) Requirement for the material to be collected and transported by the borrower himself, or by a responsible carrier of whom you approve.

b) Full insurance from the moment the picture is taken from your collection to the moment it is returned ('nail to nail' is the term often used in this context). You should have a copy of the insurance certificate in your possession before releasing the item. In assessing the value of the item, you should have consideration not simply for what the picture cost you, or even what it would cost if bought today, but what it is worth to your collection. The point made earlier, that the value of a picture may be enhanced if it is part of a series or a carefully selected collection, applies here with equal force.

c) The way the picture is mounted and hung. Some owners actually make a point of visiting the exhibition to ensure that their material is hung in conformity with their stipulations—not too near a radiator, for instance, or an open window.

d) If your picture is unmounted, you may require the borrower to pay the cost of mounting and framing. He may wish to do this in accordance with a format for the exhibition as a whole, or he may be willing to do this as suits your preference. It is usual to use perspex rather than glass when

126

loaning out a picture, so that if there is any damage it will not splinter and damage the picture. There should not be contact between the picture and the perspex; for this reason a mount is usually used to separate the two.

e) The borrower may wish to reproduce the picture in a catalogue or make it available to, say, the press, for purposes of review. It is usual to grant permission for such use, but you should ensure that due credit is given.

Mounting your own exhibitions
Most exhibitions arranged by picture libraries are made up of material within that library's possession. If you need to supplement your own material with items from other sources, then the procedure described above applies in reverse—that is, at every step you as borrower will be responsible for arranging transport, insurance, framing etc.

If you regularly mount exhibitions, there is much to be said for making or purchasing a set of standard frames and mounts, into which your pictures can be fitted for the purposes of the exhibition with a minimum of adjustment. There are many professional firms who manufacture standard frames and mounts in a range of sizes.

Publications
Every picture library is unique. Even if it does not possess unique material, it makes the material it has uniquely available, at least as far as people living locally are concerned. As a result, every library is in a position to exploit its own material, to the benefit both of itself and of those who visit the library, in a wide range of publications. These can include:

a) booklets and leaflets on specific subjects;
b) facsimiles of maps or old views of the district, suitable for framing;
c) facsimiles of old postcards and other ephemera such as posters, public notices, advertisements;
d) educational kits;
e) slide kits.

The mechanics of publishing such items would warrant a

separate publication, but in fact there are no serious problems. Most of the items fall within the competence of the average local printer, in these days of low-cost high-quality litho-processing; and for those items such as maps, which require more sophisticated treatment, there are specialist printers available with the necessary expertise for this type of work.

Publications of this sort not only provide a very valuable public service, but provide a useful additional source of revenue. Most of the cost of most publications is due to distribution and other secondary expenses: when you publish items containing your own material, and market them yourself, you can produce good quality publications at a surprisingly low price to the purchaser, and still make a useful profit for the library. You can then use the profits from one publication to finance the publication of a second, and thus in the course of time build up a collection of useful items which can often be a unique contribution to the subject. For, after all, nobody knows more about the material you have than you yourself do!

Public relations
One point has been made so repetitively through these pages that the reader may well be tired of being told how important it is that each library should be quite clear about the function it exists to perform and the public it exists to serve; my excuse must be that it is from this that almost every other decision will spring. This applies particularly to the attitude adopted towards users by the library, and it is with this fundamental consideration that our study concludes.

It is essential that every member of the library staff remembers that the purpose of the library is to serve its chosen public. The pictures exist for that public, and not the other way about.

This does not mean that, as in a shop, the customer is always right. The complexities of picture librarianship, as described in these pages, are such that most members of the public will have little idea what is entailed—as to where they should go for a particular type of service, and how they should conduct themselves when they are there. Professional picture researchers, who *do* know these things, represent only a small fraction of those who make use of the services provided by picture libraries.

What it *does* mean is that, as far as possible, the working arrangements of the library should be geared towards giving the public the service they ask for, insofar as this is consistent with the proper safeguarding of the collection. Where the public is going to be limited in the use it can make of the library—for instance, as regards access to certain types of material or the degree to which it is permitted to exploit that material—then this must be made quite clear as soon as the visitor comes through the door, if not before. For example, if the library is listed in some such publication as the *Writers and artists yearbook* or the *Picture researchers handbook*, any limitations on access or use should be made clear, to avoid wasting both the visitor's and the staff's time.

Assuming that the right person has found his way to the library, and is looking for the type of material which is likely to be found within that library, he should be encouraged to do his own research, troubling the staff as little as possible. A quick tour of the library may be necessary in some cases; simply directing him to a particular file may be all that is required in others; but a lot of time and trouble can be saved if a leaflet is available which gives the visitor basic information about the library. This could include:

Access to the library
   Who may use it
   Working hours
   Instructions about seating etc
   Details about obtaining readers' tickets etc
Access to pictures
   Basic procedure
   Using the catalogues
   Details of numbering, coding, classification
   Using the files, if open-access
Loan facilities
   Conditions
   Procedure
   Availability for reproduction

A picture is an information tool. It is doing its job only when it is being used. It is the picture librarian's duty to see that his pictures are available for use and accessible to those who wish, and have the right, to use them. It should be not only his duty, but his driving wish, to see his pictures used to the fullest extent by the greatest number of people.

ORGANISATIONS

WHILE NOT every picture library will feel the need to belong or be affiliated to all of the organisations listed here, all provide valuable services specifically related to picture librarianship and could be helpful in regard to specific aspects of the work.

Art Libraries Society (ARLIS)
Secretary: Gillian Varley, Kingston Polytechnic, Knights Park, Kingston, Surrey KT1 2QJ.
Essential organisation for all picture libraries. Primary function is disseminating information among members via bi-monthly newsletter and quarterly journal. Occasional meetings and organised visits.

British Association of Picture Libraries and Agencies (BAPLA)
PO Box 93, London NW6 5XW.
Though particularly concerned with the commercial aspect of picture librarianship, BAPLA disseminates information and establishes codes of working practice as well as recommending minimum rates. Periodic meetings, organised visits, newsletter.

Courtauld Institute of Art
20 Portman Square, London W1H OBE.
The courses in art history provided by this department of London University are probably the finest formal training a picture librarian could hope to achieve. These may be taken either as three-year undergraduate courses for BA, or as postgraduate courses (one or two years according to previous qualifications) for MA, MPhil, PhD and other courses.

The Ephemera Society
12 Fitzroy Square, London W1P 5AH.
Though largely made up of individual collectors rather than

picture libraries whose material is available to the public, this society is a useful meeting-place for all who are concerned with this increasingly important area of picture collection.

The Library Association
7 Ridgmount Street, London WC1E 7AE
Central information source for all matters relating to libraries. Its professional qualifications for Chartered Librarians are the accepted standard. Valuable library with pleasant reading room and helpful staff.

The Museums Association
87 Charlotte Street, London W1P 2BX.
Central information source for all matters relating to museums, which clearly involves a large overlap with many picture libraries. They have published a number of excellent information sheets, some of which are listed in the further reading list of this book.

FURTHER READING

THE literature of picture librarianship is almost non-existent; which is some excuse, perhaps, for the fact that the author of this book is so over-represented in this list.

Evans, Hilary *The art of picture research* David & Charles, 1979.

Evans, Hilary and Evans, Mary *The picture researchers handbook* Saturday Ventures (11 Granville Park, London SE13 7DY), 1979.

Evans, Hilary and Evans, Mary *Sources of illustration 1500-1900* Adams & Dart, 1972.

Harrison, Helen (ed) *Handbook on picture librarianship* Library Association (scheduled for publication 1980).

Lewis, John and Smith, Edwin *The graphic reproduction and photography of works of art* W S Cowell (distributed by Faber), 1969.

Museums Association *Copyright law concerning works of art: photographs and the written and spoken word*, by Charles Gibbs-Smith. (Information sheet 7), 1974.

Museums Association *Reproduction fees, photography, etc: guidelines for museums* (Information sheet 20), 1975.

Pacey, Philip (ed) *Art library manual* Bowker/ARLIS, 1977.

INDEX

135